Aegean Mercenaries in Light of the Bible

Clash of cultures in the story of David and Goliath

Simona Rodan

Archaeopress Publishing

Archaeopress Publishing Ltd
Gordon House
276 Banbury Road
Oxford OX2 7ED

www.archaeopress.com

ISBN 978 1 78491 106 5
ISBN 978 1 78491 107 2 (e-Pdf)

© Archaeopress and S Rodan 2015

Drawings © Margalit Levitan

All rights reserved. No part of this book may be reproduced, stored in retrieval system, or transmitted, in any form or by any means, electronic, mechanical, photocopying or otherwise, without the prior written permission of the copyright owners.

Printed and bound in Great Britain by Marston Book Services Ltd, Oxfordshire

This book is available direct from Archaeopress or from our website www.archaeopress.com

In memory of Gershon Argov, a teacher and educator

Contents

List of Figures iii

Introduction 1
   1. Aegean mercenaries and their role in the Near East and in Egypt since the 8th century BCE 4
   2. Aegean mercenaries in the Bible 9

A. Research approaches to the story of the duel between David and Goliath and the figure of Goliath 12
   A.1. The story of the duel has no historical basis 13
   A.2. The story was created and edited after David's period (8th century BCE till the Second Temple period) 13
   A.3. The story was written around the time of David 21

B. Who were the opponents in the duel and when did the event take place? 27

C. The defensive armament of Goliath and conclusions about his identity and name 29
   C.1. The ethos of military arms and shields in Greece and Israel 29
   C.2. The development of hoplite armor 31
   C.3. Comparison between the armor of Goliath and the hoplite armor 40
      C.3.1. The armor of Goliath and its heavy weight 40
      C.3.2. The shield bearer of Goliath 40
      C.3.3. The helmet of Goliath 41
   C.4. Diversionary tactics 42
   C.5. How did 'γυαλαθώραξ' turn into 'Goliath' 47

D. The name is the message: four proofs 50
   D.1. Parallel instances of a military equipment item turning into a personal name or epithet 50
   D.2. The Philistine warrior was nameless 52
   D.3. There are multiple 'Goliaths' 53
   D.4. Names of additional biblical foreign warriors which derive from military terms 54

E. Who was the enemy represented by Goliath? The Saites and their Aegean mercenaries 61

F. Saite-Aegean myths in a distorted mirror 73
   F.1. The armor and helmet that saved the nation and its king 73
   F.2. Deliverance of the army by a hero in a duel with an armed giant 79

G. The story of the duel in light of the biblical attitude to the Babylonian exiles and the Egyptian diaspora 82

Conclusion 98

Bibliography 103
    A. Literary sources and commentaries.. 103
    B. Modern studies 105
    Abbreviations 112

List of Figures

Fig. 1. The Aegean basin. iv
Fig. 2. Land of Israel in the Late Monarchic Period. 2
Fig. 3. Ancient Egypt in the Late Period. 3
Fig. 4. Bronze 'bell corselette' and high-crest helmet. 33
Fig. 5. Centauromachia. 34
Fig. 6. Achilles killing the Amazon Queen Penthesilea. 35
Fig. 7. Combat of hoplites. 36
Fig. 8. Bronze plate cuirass. 37
Fig. 9. Menelaos pursuing Helen. 38
Fig. 10. Bronze Corinthian helmet and pair of greaves. 39
Fig. 11. Hoplite. 43
Fig. 12. Archer and combat of Hoplites. 44
Fig. 13. Bust of Pericles. 45
Fig. 14. Silver Phoenician bowl. 66
Fig. 15. Assyrian soldier with hoplite gear. 67
Fig. 16. Aegean hoplite on an Ionian amphora from Daphnae. 75
Fig. 17. Aegean hoplite engraved on a relief from Naukratis. 76
Fig. 18. Carian skyphos from Naukrtis. 77
Fig. 19. Carian stela from Saqqara. 94
Fig. 20. Ionian amphora from Thebes. 95

Fig. 1. The Aegean basin.
Drawing: Margalit Levitan.

Introduction

Herodotus relates that during the reign of Psammeticus I, ruler of a district of the Delta in Egypt, Ionian and Carian sea pirates came ashore and began pillaging. They were armed with bronze weapons and armor that the Egyptians had never seen before. Psammeticus understood that they were the realization of the oracle he had received that that brazen men would come from the sea and make him become the sole rulers of Egypt, and he hired their services (Herodotus II.152-154). The story has a legendary color, but it finds support in the inscription of Ashurbanipal, King of Assyria, dated to 643/2 BCE which reports that Gyges, King of Lydia, sent mercenaries to help Psammeticus who had rebelled against him (Prism A, in: Tadmor & Cogan 1977: 79). The Greek mercenaries gradually became the decisive factor in the wars that were waged in the Near East and in the Greek world during the Archaic, Classical and Hellenistic periods. Although they were few in number, temporary residents, and cultural inferiors in the countries in which they served, they were considered as having the power to determine the fates of armies and peoples, to elevate and to overthrow rulers and kingdoms. This was due to their technological advantages – heavy weapons and metal armor – and to their skills in warfare. In Greek these foot soldiers with heavy weapons were called 'hoplites' from the word ὅπλα (arms, weapons).

The mercenaries participated in the wars between the great powers of the Near East which were also fateful for the Kingdom of Judah. Pharaoh Necho II who led his mercenaries into battle against Assyria and Babylon in 609 BCE, killed Josiah, King of Judah during the course of his campaign and crowned Jehoiakim as his loyal client king. After the battle, Babylon gained hegemony over the Near East, but the kings of Judah, under the influence of Egypt that promised them military assistance, rebelled repeatedly against Babylon. Pharaoh Hophra (Greek: Apries) had tens of thousands of mercenaries (Herodotus II.163). He was an ally of Zedekiah, King of Judah, and came to his aid during the siege that Nebuchadnezzar II imposed on Jerusalem. But he failed and retreated (Jeremiah, 37-39). In 586 the city was conquered and destroyed, and the Jews were exiled to Babylon.

Many of those who remained behind in Judah migrated to Egypt, and this was the beginning of the great Jewish diaspora there. They settled in the cities where the mercenaries dwelt such as Tahpanhes (Tell Daphnae), Noph (Memphis), Migdol (Tell el-Heir) and Syene/Swene (today Aswan). The Jews also served as mercenaries in Egypt. Already in the days of Psammeticus I, mercenaries were sent from Judah to help him in his wars against the Nubians. A settlement of Jewish mercenaries was stationed in Yeb (Elephantine) on the Nubian border until the 4th century BCE (see below).

In 532 BCE the Jewish exiles in Babylon received permission from Cyrus, King of Persia, to return to their homeland. They set up their temple and reinstated the fundamental elements of their faith. The later prophets were active during this period and a large part of the Bible was composed at that time. This was a historiographic composition with strong political and cultural positions towards every factor and event in the international arena.

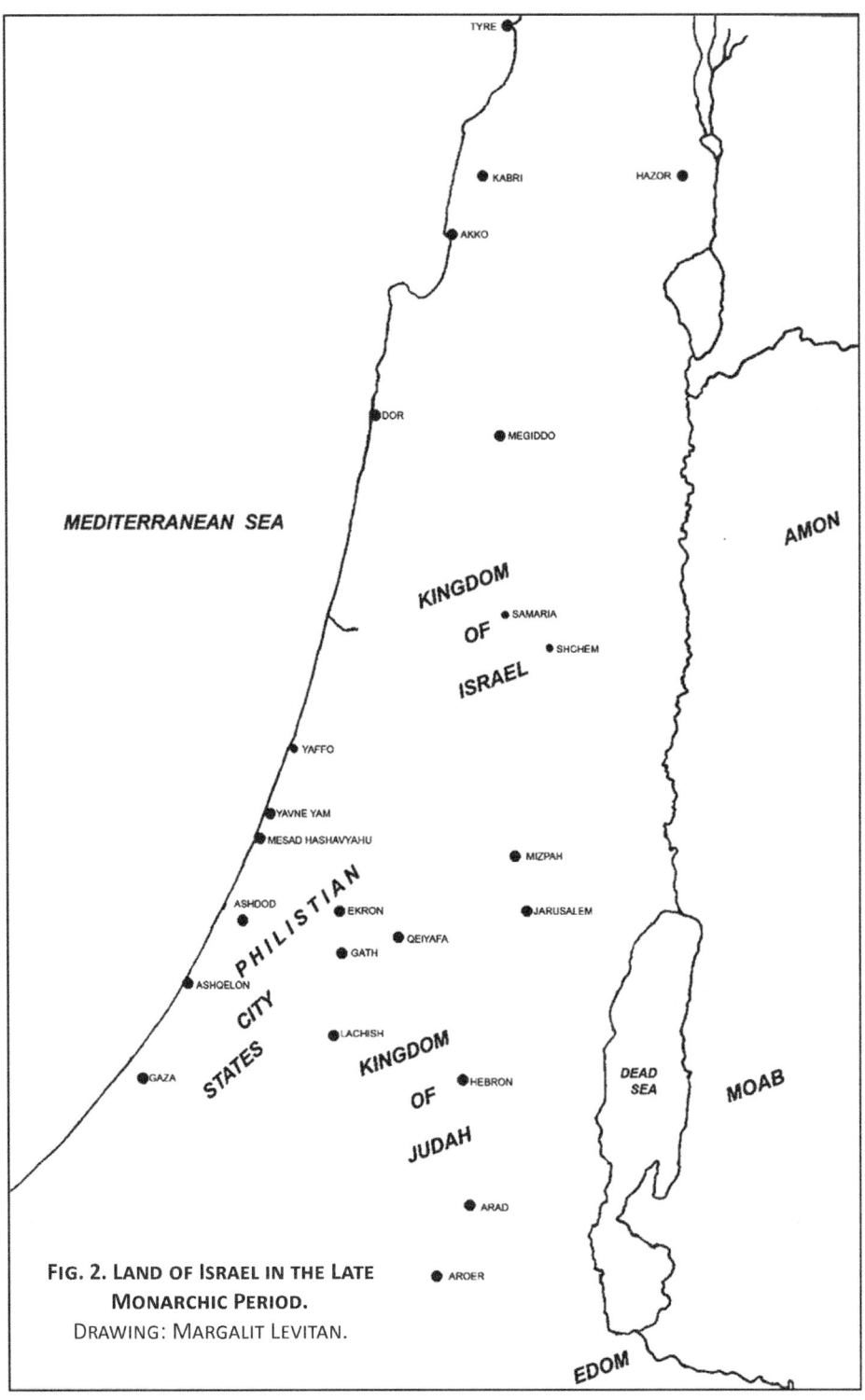

Fig. 2. Land of Israel in the Late Monarchic Period.
Drawing: Margalit Levitan.

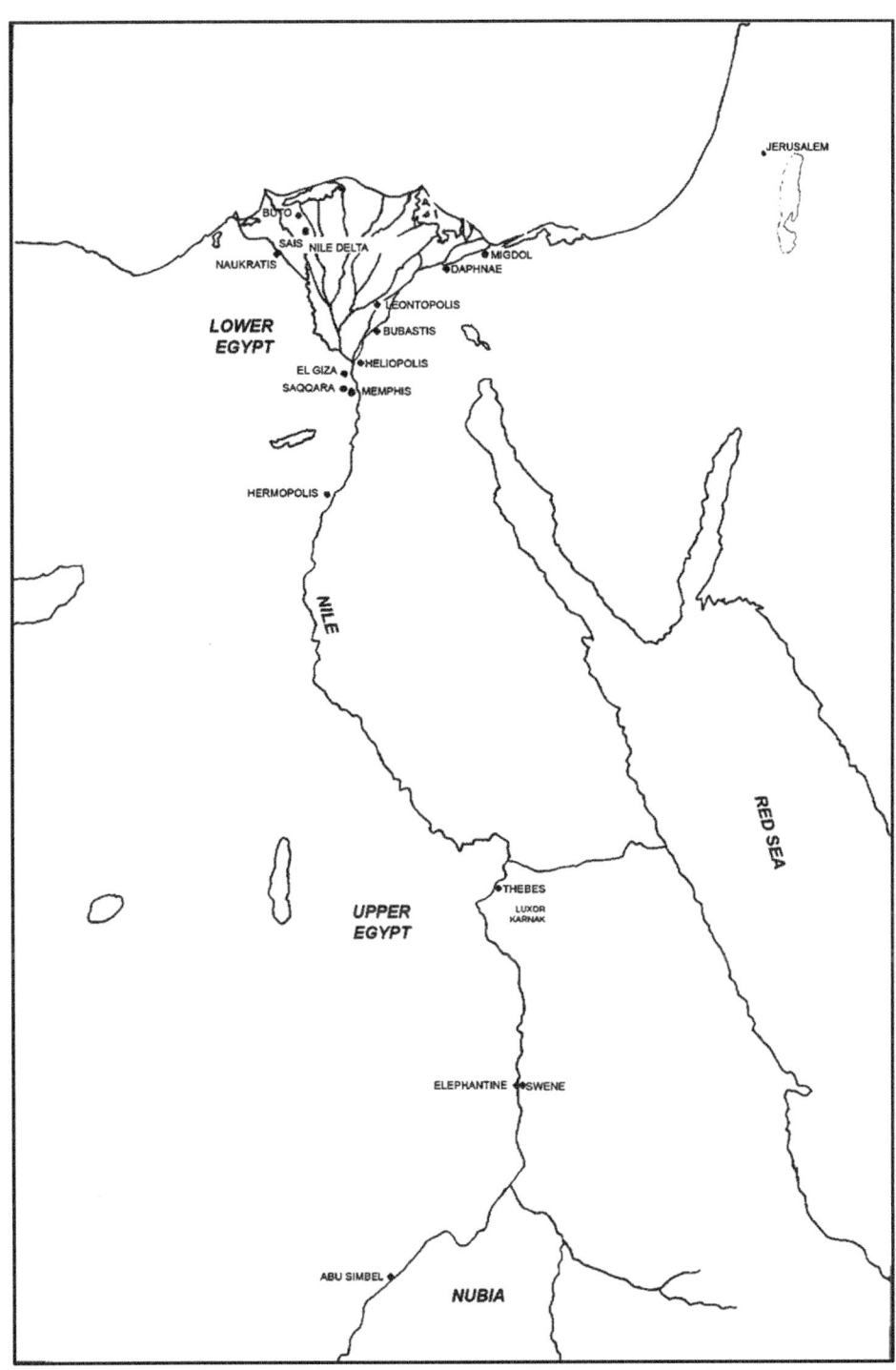

Fig. 3. Ancient Egypt in the Late Period.
Drawing: Margalit Levitan.

What was its attitude towards the mercenaries and the constant encounters with them? It is strange that they are rarely mentioned. More is told about them at the beginning of the monarchy at the start of the first millennium BCE, and less at the end of the monarchy and the days of exile when their numbers and influence had increased very much.

1. Aegean mercenaries and their role in the Near East and in Egypt since the 8th century BCE

War was a central value in Greek society in ancient times. Plato presented it as a natural situation in which every country was in perpetual state of war with another, and therefore ειρήνη (peace) was a word empty of content (*Laws*, 1.625-1.626). In his Republic, the citizens received military education (*Republic*, II.373; V.466). The Athenians raised Eirene to the level of divinity only when they were exhausted in the Peloponnesian wars, and Aristophanes and Euripides presented her as an ideal that one should aspire to.[1] During the Archaic period aristocrats exhibited in their homes their metal-made arms to represent a sense of power to viewers. At first personal weapons used to be buried in the graves of their owners, but this custom ceased so that they could remain in use. Weaponry was sometimes gifted to temples as a thanksgiving offering or as a request for mercy, and warriors often dedicated arms from the spoils of victories. The temples themselves were centers of the metal industry and of mercenary recruitment (Morgan 2001: 20-27).

Initially, mercenaries from the Greek world were active outside it. The Bible relates that the kings of Israel and Judah employed Hittite,[2] Cretan, Philistine and Carian mercenaries, and the Arad *Ostraca* mention the Kittim (from Kition in Cyprus) (Aharoni 1981: 12-28, 145). Scholars are divided in their opinion about the extent of activity of the Aegean mercenaries in Assyria and Babylon (see below). But in Egypt their numbers reached tens of thousands in the 6th century BCE (Herodotus II.163). They helped Psammeticus I to oust the 25th 'Nubian' dynasty and then to liberate himself from Assyrian domination and unify Egypt. With their assistance, his descendants fought against the Nubians and the Babylonians, conquered Philistia, Judah, and Phoenicia, and suppressed internal revolts. From the inscriptions of mercenaries discovered in Abu Simbel in Egypt it appears that they originated from various cities in Ionia, Caria and Rhodes (Meiggs & Lewis: 1969 nos. 7, 7b, 7f, 7g).

Assyria, Egypt, Babylon and Persia were large empires with rich and densely populated cities, magnificent temples where ancient and awe-inspiring cultic rites were practiced, and where literary and scientific creativity flourished. At the beginning of the Archaic period, the Aegean world that had emerged from a period of 'Dark Ages' decline and detachment was still divided into small and impoverished political units. Urban settlements were few

---

[1] Aristophanes, 'Peace'. Euripides, 'Orestes', 1682-3; idem, 'Bacchae', 419-420. Eirene was previously considered as one of the seasons of the year (identified with the harvest season during which war was avoided). In the 5th century BCE she was presented only twice in art, and in Athens a public cult to Eirene was established only in the year 376/5 BCE (Cornelius Nepos, 'Timotheus' 2.2; Smith 2005: 211-231).

[2] 'Hittites' in the Bible are of the Neo-Hittite/Neo-Luwian kingdoms that arose in the north of Syria and in Southern Anatolia after the break up of the Hittite Empire at the end of the Bronze Age. David and Solomon made alliances, trade agreements and marriage ties with their rulers (1 Kings 10:29; 1 Kings 11:1; 2 Chronicles 1:17; Zinger 2009: 106-107).

and lacked planning. The temples and statues of the gods were small and simple, built of wood. Contacts with the East, (together with two other phenomena – the rise of the *polis*, the city-state type of government instead of local kings, and the colonization movement), created an enormous upsurge among the Greeks in their political, economic, social and cultural development. From the 9th to the 7th century BCE, Greek traders (mainly from Euboia on the Greek mainland) were active in Northern Syria, as testified by the large quantity of imported Greek vessels discovered in the al-Mina excavations in the Orontes estuary. A smaller quantity from the 7th century BCE was found in Ras al-Bassit and Tell Sukas. Traders bought ivories, seals and bronze vessels in Northern Syria and sold them throughout the Mediterranean area. During this period, the Ionians acted as merchants and pirates along the shores of Cilicia, Syria and Phoenicia. The kings of Assyria who dominated that area from 732 BCE, apparently recruited them as mercenaries (Luraghi 2006: 30-40). In the course of the 7th and 6th centuries BCE the Pharaohs of Egypt also recruited Aegean mercenaries, and Aegean merchants were allowed to settle in the city of Naucratis. They adopted some elements of the Egyptian religion and art (Herodotus II.61; Livingston 2000; Villing & Schlozhauer 2006: 5-8) (see below). Aegean mercenaries also served Babylon, and through them the knowledge fruits of the highly developed cultures in the Near East and Egypt reached the Aegean world (Burkert 1992; Knapp 2002; Raaflaub 2004). They contributed to the formation of the Greek alphabet and the development of science and of epic and lyric literature. Artists and craftsmen adopted the Mesopotamian and Egyptian artistic techniques and methods of representation, and developed a new and unique style. This period was thus called the 'Orientalizing Period'.[3]

In the mid-6th century BCE, the hiring of mercenaries spread to the Aegean world as well. In mainland Greece and in Sicily, and in many other *poleis*, tyrants hired them to gain sovereignty and to obtain personal protection, such as Polycrates in Samos, Pisistratus in Athens, Hippocrates and Gelon in Gela and in Syracuse. The spread of coins in the Greek world made payments easier (Knapp 2002: 192-194; Trundle 2004: 83-84). At the end of the 5th century BCE, the demand for them also increased in the Persian Empire, and large armies of tens of thousands of mercenaries were engaged in campaigns of conquest, to repel invasions, and in civil wars.[4]

Most of the Greek mercenaries fought as hoplites (Diodorus Siculus 15.44.1-3) and they were much in demand. There was no lack of lightly armed warriors in the Near East and in Egypt (see for example, Herodotus IX.63.2). We shall expand upon the style of armor

---

[3] Knapp (2002) and Raaflaub (2004) pointed out the key role of the mercenaries in the connections between the Greek world and the developed cultures of the Near East and Egypt. Boardman (1997) indicated the various expressions of Eastern influence on Greek pottery in various regions of Greece. Livingston (2000) drew attention to the adoption of motifs from Egyptian architecture and sculpture, such as the volutes and lotus in the Ionic capitals, and also the labyrinth by the Ionians in Egypt and in Asia Minor. Burkert mentioned the Mesopotamian and Egyptian influences on Greek philosophy, literature, and religion. The mercenaries were the channel through which Akkadian words from the military sphere were borrowed by the Greek language such as harpe (sword), macha (war), skylon (plunder), as well as divination through the entrails of sacrificial animals. The practice of liver divinations was transmitted from Mesopotamia to Caria and spread throughout Greece (Burkert 1992: 39-40, 48-49).

[4] Cyrus II in 401 BCE hired about 11,000 mercenaries in order to seize the throne; Artaxerxes III in 380 BCE engaged between 12 and 20 thousand mercenaries from mainland Greece to invade Egypt. Darius III employed 50,000 of them against Alexander of Macedon, who also recruited 30,000 mercenaries to conquer the Persian Empire. Tens of thousands of mercenaries served the Pharaohs of Egypt in the 4th century BCE.

and warfare of the hoplites later on. Their weapons and shields were expensive, and in Greek society they were assigned a respected position in the community. In Athens in 594 BCE, Solon conducted reforms that divided society into classes according to property and military service. The ζευγέται (landowners) who could finance the cost of weapons and shield and fight like hoplites were given the right to be elected to political positions (see also Thucydides 8.97.1). Members of the lower class - θέτες (the poor), who could not afford this, participated only in general assemblies (they could serve as oarsmen in warships and receive wages).[5] The hired mercenaries depended on their arms and armor for their livelihood. Most of them came to their employers already equipped (for example, *Anabasis*, 1.2.4) but sometimes they received their arms from them. Dionysius of Syracuse, for example, produced thousands of bronze armaments for them (Diodorus (16.42.2-3).

Where did the mercenaries come from and what made them enlist in a foreign army and endanger their lives in a strange country? Some scholars believe that their numbers were not many at first, and that they were members of the social elite in their native countries which they had to abandon in the wake of civil wars. This was the way to survive abroad, and it suited their education and trained abilities. In this way they received shelter, livelihood and an opportunity to excel in acts of bravery, and to return to their homeland crowned with glory (Bettalli 1995: 24-27; Trundle 1999: 130; Kaplan 2002: 236-241). For example, Alcaeus, the poet, and his brother Antimenidas, who were exiled from Mytilene; the former became a mercenary of Lydia and the latter a mercenary of Babylon (see below). Other scholars believe that mercenaries arrived in groups and in large numbers, since there was no demand for lone soldiers, and that they came not only from among the nobility but also from peripheral regions in the Greek world (Luraghi 2006: 23-24).[6] Mercenaries also came from tribal communities outside the *poleis* (Trundle 2004: 139). Their service gave them the opportunity to become wealthy. Antimenidas, and also Pedon, the mercenary of Psammeticus I, amassed precious objects (Fr. 48 apud: Campbell 1982: 385-386. *SEG* XXXVII, 1987: 994). Xenophon (who had enlisted in the service of Cyrus II in 401 BCE) acquired many possessions, and on his return he bought lands and built a temple to Artemis (*Anabasis*, 5.3.7-8).

Many of the mercenaries enlisted for Φιλία (fellowship) and for ξενία (guest-friendship) which were of great importance in Greek society. The *philia*, along with family relationships, were the basis for the status of the citizen in his community. If he went out to fight in a foreign country, his fellow companions would join him. Greeks formed companionships even with strangers. Pigres the Carian was the close companion of Psammeticus I (Polyaenus, 7.3). Cyrus II had *philia* and *xenia* ties with a number of

---

[5] Van Wees claimed that in Athens θέτες with a certain income could enlist as hoplites (Van Wees 2001: 45-71). The authorities sometimes provided poor recruits with light weapons and shields (Trundle 2004: 118-119).
[6] Kaplan brings evidence of their noble origins such as the bronze hoplite armor and weapon which was beyond the means of ordinary people and required much training in order to use it skillfully; the ability to contact employers and to function in alien societies; and their level of education which is reflected in the inscriptions they left. Against this, Luraghi asserts that the soldiers in the rear ranks of the army did not need full armor, and that professional soldiers invested in arms that could also be obtain from the spoils of war (Kaplan 2002: 230, 341; Luraghi 2006: 25). It is clear that the masses of mercenaries in the later periods did not come only from among the nobility. During the days of Isocrates and Demosthenes, they were recruited even from amongst the poor, the vagrants and the destitute refugees (Isocrates 4.168; 8.44; 5.121; Demosthenes 4.46; 14.31; 12.27).

nobles in Greece, and they recruited thousands of mercenaries for him. Among the elite, *xenia* ties were formed between those who did not belong to the same ethnic background, tribe or *polis*. This included hospitality, the exchange of ceremonial gifts, mutual defense and assistance, which passed down in legacy to descendants.[7] Xenophon enlisted in the army of Cyrus because of his *xenia* ties with a mercenary and his hopes of becoming a *philos* of Cyrus who was famous for his generous remunerations (*Anabasis*, 3.1.4). The first mercenaries created *xenia* ties with the local aristocracy and laid the groundwork for their descendants who inherited their profession. Mercenaries were often accompanied by their wives and children, and it was common for brothers, fathers and sons to fight together (Isocrates 4.168. Xenophon, *Anabasis*, 1.4.8; 5.3.1).

The mercenaries were subject to the employer and worked for wages. This contradicted the Greek aristocratic-heroic ideal of freedom and economic independence (Trundle 2004: 19). The vague terminology in Greek for mercenaries reflects the cognitive dissonance that prevailed with regard to them. At first they used the term 'επίκουρος' which in the Iliad means a side-warrior, an auxiliary, such as Sarpedon the Lician, without any mention of recompense. But from the words of Archilochus the poet[8] of the mid-7th century BCE, it appears that it also means a professional mercenary soldier: 'και δη 'πικουρος ὥστε Καρ κεκλήσομαι' (I shall be called an 'επίκουρος' like a Carian)(*CURFRAG.tlg-0232.25*). 'παιδεύειν, σκοπεῖν χρὴ μὴ οὐκ ἐν τῷ Καρὶ ὑμῖν ὁ κίνδυνος κινδυνεύηται, ἀλλ' ἐν τοῖς ὑέσι τε καὶ ἐν τοῖς τῶν φίλων παισί' (you must beware lest you try your experiment, not on a 'Carian', but on your sons and the children of your friends) (Plato, *Laches* 187b). The Carians were considered to have been the first mercenaries in the Greek world (Eforos, *FGrH* 70 F 12). Alcaeus called Antimenidas a σύμμαχος (ally, side-warrior) of the Babylonians. In the 5th century BCE a new term appeared: *xenos* (ξένος) which means stranger, guest, and also implies the nobility of a foreign warrior who offers assistance because of *xenia* ties. Xenophon called his Greek colleagues ξένοι while the mercenaries of the enemy army or those of barbaric origins he termed μισθοφόροι (payment receivers) derived from the word μίσθος, payment (*Anabasis*, 4.3.4; 7.8.15). The euphemistic camouflage was gradually removed, and in the 4th century BCE it was already the practice to use the unambiguous term στρατιώτης μισθοφόρος for the professional hired soldier.

Although the mercenaries presented themselves in a noble and heroic light, their reputation was that of greedy opportunists and cowards. Archilochus rejected the opportunism of the mercenaries: 'ἐπίκουρος ἀνήρ τόσσον φίλος ἔσκε μάχηται' (the epikouros is your friend as long as he fights at your side) (*CURFRAG.tlg-0323.14*). He was a professional soldier, but he fought only for the sake of Paros, his homeland, and claimed that he was indifferent to the golden treasures of Gyges (*CURFRAG.tlg-0323.26*). Herodotus and Aristotle described how mercenaries assisted the tyrant Peisistratus to subject the

---

[7] In the Iliad, Diomedes and Glaucus met in combat, but when they discovered that their ancestors had been xenoi, they did not fight each other but exchanged gifts (VI: 215-233). On philia and xenia among mercenaries, see Trundle 1999; 2004. In Greek society in general, see G. Herman, *Ritualized Friendship and the Greek City*, 1987.

[8] Archilochus was a professional soldier, as can be seen from his many sayings, e.g. 'Εἰμὶ δ'ἐγώ θεράπων μὲν Ἐνυαλίοιο ἄνακτος, Καὶ Μουσέων ἐρατὸν δῶρον ἐπιστάμενος' (I am the servant of the Lord Ares and skilled in the lovely gift of the Muses) (*CURFRAG.tlg-032.1*).

Athenians (Herodotus I.61. Aristotle, *Athenaean Constitution*, 15.1-3). They tended to change sides in wars. The mercenaries of Pelopidas were bribed by his enemy Ptolemy the Macedonian in 368 BCE and went over to his side (Plutarch, *Pelopidas*, 27.3). Aristotle notes that professional soldiers had a greater tendency to flee than citizens who were prepared to sacrifice their lives (*Nicomachean Ethics*, 3.8.9). On the other hand, there were also instances of loyalty. The colleagues of Phanes of Halicarnasus, who had betrayed Pharaoh Amasis II and incited Cambyses II to invade Egypt, slaughtered his children before his eyes and drank their blood. The punishment was not for having endangered them but because he brought war to Egypt (Herodotus III.4-11).

Remuneration for mercenaries differed from place to place and from period to period. The first mercenaries in Egypt received land as well as those in Sicily (Herodotus II.54. Diodorus 14.78.1-3). They were also paid with food such as wheat, meat, and wine (which was mentioned as an allocation to the Kittim in the Arad *Ostraca*), or with χρήματα (money) in order to hire them. The νομίσματα (coins) appeared in Lydia around the year 600 BCE, but in the Near East and Egypt they continued even later on to use payment methods such as expensive metals by weight (Bettalli 1995: 78-79; Trundle 2004: 82-90; Sullivan 2011: 34-38). To finance the mercenaries, mines were exploited, taxes were levied, property was expropriated, and temple treasures were plundered (Herodotus III.89-117. Xenophon, *Hellenica*, 7.1.45-46. Diodorus 16.30.1). Officers earned four times more, and commanders twice more than ordinary soldiers (Xenophon, *Anabasis*, 7.1.6). Remuneration for mercenaries gradually lessened, and in the 4th century BCE they lived from hand to mouth. Their main income was from spoils and plunder, from the sale of slaves, and the extortion of ransom. A vicious circle developed in which employers initiated wars in order to pay the mercenaries from the spoils (Trundle 2004: 91-101). The prophet Ezekiel relates that in the year 571 BCE Nebuchadnezzar failed in his attempt to conquer Tyre and was therefore forced to conquer Egypt in order to pay his soldiers: 'Nebuchadnezzar king of Babylon caused his army to serve a great service against Tyre … yet he had no wages for his army in Tyre for the work that they had done … Therefore behold I shall give Nebuchadnezzar …the land of Egypt, and he shall take her multitude and plunder her spoils, and pillage her booty, and it shall be the wages for his army' (Ezekiel 29:18-20). This testifies to the service of mercenaries in the Babylonian army. The payment they expected was captives they sold into slavery, spoils and plunder. The mercenaries were constantly forced to search for employment and livelihood. The mercenaries of Cyrus, after his death in the battle against Artaxerxes, tried to persuade Artaxerxes to recruit them and to invade Egypt with their assistance (*Anabasis*, 2.5.11-14).

Xenophon portrayed the mercenary warriors, their motives and their character, such as Clearchus the adventurer and lover of wars, Proxenus the ambitious, and Menon the avaricious (*Anabasis*, 2.6.1-9). Mercenaries were obedient and loyal to their commander as long as they trusted in his success. If they suspected that he would fail, they deserted or even assassinated him (*Anabasis*, 1.3.1-2). Sometimes they felt more loyalty towards their employers or commanders than towards their homeland. Proxenus declared that he loved Cyrus more than his native country, and Clearchus said that he would never prefer barbarians to his Greek colleagues who were for him 'συμμάχους καὶ φίλους καὶ πατρίδα' (companions in arms and friends and homeland) (*Anabasis*, 1.3.5; 3.1.4). The mercenary warriors were often accused of betraying their homeland. Thus, for example, Xenophon and Ificrates stood trial and exiled; the former because of serving Cyrus, and the latter because he served Cotys, King of Thrace who fought against Athens (Demosthenes, *Against Aristocrates*, 23.130-132). Yet their activities abroad sometimes served the interests of their homeland as well. Conon of Athens commanded the Persian fleet in the Battle of Cnidus in 394 BCE, defeated the Spartan fleet, and eliminated the hegemony of Sparta over the sea.

The Aegean mercenaries did not serve in mixed ethnic units. From the Abu Simbel inscription, the mercenaries of Psammeticus belonged to a unit called αλλογλοσσοι (speakers of a foreign language), and it seems this was how the Egyptians named them (Malkin, 'Pan-Hellenism', 2003: 92). Cyrus II also kept them apart from his soldiers. The Greeks themselves took care to preserve their prestige as elite units. Xenophon tells about a Lydian mercenary who disguised himself as a Boeotian, and was ejected. He spoke the Boeotian language but they found him out by the earring holes in his earlobes 'because the natives were famous for their feminine indulgences', contrary to the Greek masculine ideal (*Anabasis*, 3.1.26-27). The Greeks were proud of their national identity, and their commanders used to lecture them about their superiority to the barbarians which was due to their courage and freedom (*Anabasis*, 3.2.11-12).

2. Aegean mercenaries in the Bible

The attitude towards warfare and arms in the Bible is ambiguous. On one hand, peace is presented as the supreme ideal. In the end of days all nations would stream to the Temple in Jerusalem and be educated in accordance with its doctrine. As a result: '…They shall beat their swords into plowshares, and their spears into pruning hooks. Nation shall not lift up sword against nation, neither shall they learn war any more' (Isaiah 2:4; Michah 4:3). God did not allow David to build him a temple because he was a man of war and had shed blood. The Temple was erected by Solomon, whose name was derived from the word 'Shalom' – peace, and during his reign peace prevailed. In building of the Temple and in the holy services it was forbidden to use iron tools since this metal was used to produce weaponry (1 Kings 6-7; 1 Chronicles 22: 8-10; 2 Chronicles 28:3). On the other hand, they were forced to compromise with the reality of frequent wars. Paradoxically, the Temple served as an arsenal for weapons. David dedicated the sword of Goliath to the tabernacle, and when he fled from Saul he took it back from there. His arms were kept in the Temple and served for the overturning of the regime about 120 years later. Precious armaments were exhibited in the Temple such as the shields of gold that were taken as spoils by Shishak, King of Egypt (1 Samuel 21:10; 1 Kings 14:26; 2 Kings 11:10).

The Aegean mercenaries are interwoven the history of the kingdoms of Israel and Judah from the beginning of the monarchic period until the destruction of the First Temple (c.1020 – 586 BCE). In the Bible those who assisted the Jewish people are depicted in a positive light, while those who served the enemy were described negatively. The early monarchic period was one of unrest during which the Land of Israel and its surroundings formed into national states that frequently fought among themselves. The struggle for control over the country extended mainly between the Israelites and the Philistines.[9] The first mercenaries described in the Bible were – unexpectedly – Judaeans: David and his men who served ruler of Aegean origin: Achish, the Philistine King of Gath (1 Samuel 21-27; 29-30). How did David, a member of a respected family in Judah, become a mercenary of the enemy of his people? He had attained a high position in the court of King Saul thanks to the warlike skills he demonstrated in the duel with Goliath and as a military commander against the Philistines. But his success aroused envy and fear in the heart of Saul who tried to kill him. David fled and gathered members of his family around him as well as those who were persecuted like himself or in debt: 'When his brothers and his father's house heard it, they went down to him there. And everyone who was in distress and everyone who was in debt, and every man who was discontented, gathered around him, and he became a captain over them' (1 Samuel 22:1-2). They lived on their swords, roamed through Judah, protected farmers from Philistine raiders and in return requisitioned food from them. Saul tried repeatedly to capture him, and when David discovered that the inhabitants of the cities Ke'ilah and Ziph plotted to hand him over, he was forced to go over to Philistia and to hire himself out as a mercenary to Achish: 'And Achish believed David, saying: He has made his people in Israel to abhor him, and will be my servant forever' (ibid., 27:12). He had ordered him to attack his homeland, but David attacked the Amalekites, the Gerizites, and the Geshurites, the enemies of Israel, and reported to him that he had invaded Judah. As reward, David and his men found refuge and patronage and amassed much wealth from the spoils of his raids and the plundering. David received the city of Ziklag from Achish, just as Pedon received a city from Psammeticus I. His warriors regarded him as responsible for their lives and property. When they discovered that the Amalekites had overrun Ziklag and captured their wives, children and all that they owned, they wanted to kill David. He set out to fight the Amalekites and brought back the captives. He then introduced a fair method of dividing the spoils that became the standard practice. Those who remained behind to stay by the supplies would receive the same recompense as those who went down to battle. David and his 600 men were a separate unit in the army of Achish. They were demanded to join him in the battle of the Philistines against Saul

---

[9] The Philistines were part of a group of peoples mentioned in Egyptian sources such as the wall reliefs of Medinet Habu, Papyrus Harris, and the Onomasticon of Amenope. According to them, 'foreign countries [peoples] made a conspiracy in their islands'. They attacked and destroyed the Hittite empire and city states in Cilicia and northern Syria. They invaded Egypt and fought against it on sea and land. Rameses III (1186-1154 BCE) defeated them and they settled with his permission in Canaan. Other groups, the Tjeker and Sherden had colonies there. Many modern researchers call these groups the 'Sea People' as Gaston Maspero called them in 1889. In the Bible there are contradictory statements about the origins of the Philistines: from Egypt (Genesis 10:13-14; I Chronicles 1:11-12), from Crete (Amos 7:9; Jeremiah 47:4; Ezekiel 25:16). But in the research it is accepted that the Philistine words mentioned there originated in Asia Minor, such as kupahi – כּוֹבַע, tyrannoi - סְרָנִים. According to writers from Asia Minor, Xanthus of Lydia (5th century BCE) and Ctesias of Cnidus (5th to 4th centuries BCE), Ashqelon was founded by Mopsus of Phrygia and Askalos of Lydia. Writers of the Byzantine period such as Stephanus of Byzantium and Marcus Diaconus say that Cretans settled in Gaza. During the Roman and Byzantine periods, a pantheon of Cretan gods existed in Gaza such as Minos, Marnas/Zeus Cretagenes. Scholars such as S. Sheratt, M. Yon and A. Gilboa regard them as the local population from Northern Syria or Cyprus. E. Stern and T. Dothan think their origins were in the west part of the Aegean Sea, and according to Zinger (1989), in Northern Syria and Western Anatolia. Yasur-Landau believes they came from the Dodecanese islands or the Anatolian coast near them, and that they arrived in Egypt or Canaan by land. There was no violent occupation and settlement, but rather co-existence with the Canaanites (2010: 162-163, 192; 2012). Ugarit and Hittite documents of the Bronze Age testify to their connections with Ahhiyawa in the Peloponnesus or the Mycenaean world. During the Iron Age the Kingdom of Ahhiyawa existed in Anatolia and its name preserved the memory of its origins. In Northern Syria there existed a Wadashtini/Padashtini Kingdom (Palestine?). See note 15.

in Gilboa. But when the other 'Sarnei plishtim' – leaders of the other Philistine cities saw David, they accused him of intending to betray them and expelled him from their ranks. Achish, who loved David and had heaped gifts upon him as was customary in the Greek *xenia*, apologized to him for this. It seems that this relationship allowed David after he was crowned king to recruit hundreds of mercenaries from Gath. The friendship continued during the days of his son Solomon. It can be concluded from the case with the servants of Shimei the son of Gera, David's enemy, who fled and found refuge with Achish (1 Samuel 16:3-13; 1 Kings 2:36-46). There were also some elements of *philia* and *xenia* in the relations between David and Jonathan the son of Saul, which overrode the ties of family, tribe and status. Jonathan had given David his garments and his arms, and they made a promise that they would bequeath their relationship of loyalty, assistance and protection to their descendants (1 Samuel 20:16, 42; 1 Kings 2:39-41).

The Israelite army during the period of the Judges and Saul was composed of farmer fighters who were recruited during times of emergency. David recruited elite units from the Aegean mercenaries, perhaps in view of his experience with Achish. They were called according to their ethnic origins (Hittites, Cherethites, Gittites) and not 'mercenaries', in order to blur the fact they were paid soldiers and to emphasize that they served for love. Uriah the Hittite was an exemplary model of loyalty and courage in the Bible. He settled in Jerusalem and married the Jewess Bathsheba, but fell victim to the betrayal of David who fell in love with her. She conceived with David, and when Uriah refused his offer to return home and to attend to his wife, he sent him to the battle front and caused his death. The punishment of David and Bathsheba was the death of their child, but their second son Solomon became the King of Israel. The mercenaries of David remained at his side when his son Absalom and most of the people rebelled against him. We shall see below how the Carians also saved his dynasty from extinction.

David is not presented in the Bible as an outstanding example of loyalty between mercenary and employer. But his loyalty to his people, his homeland and his ruler are emphasized, which he maintained even when he was pursued and exiled by them.

Aegean mercenaries are also mentioned at the end of the Judaean monarchy and the Babylonian exile in the books of the prophets Jeremiah and Ezekiel. This time they represent the repressive powers, Babylon and especially Egypt. They are scornfully termed 'mercenaries' with emphasis on their work and wages, and are described as poor fighters, cowardly and defeated. In modern research a new assumption was recently raised that there is another coded reference to the Aegean mercenaries in the story of the duel between David and Goliath which is described in the Book of Samuel.

A. Research approaches to the story of the duel between David and Goliath and the figure of Goliath

There are two versions in the Bible for the duel that Goliath the Philistine conducted against an Israelite hero. The most famous, detailed and accepted version is the one found in the Masoretic Text (MT) of I Samuel 17, according to which he was vanquished by David in the Valley of Elah. Goliath is described in verses 4-7: 'And there went out a champion [lit. 'the man in the space between'] out of the camp of the Philistines, named Goliath of Gath, whose height was six cubits and a span. And he had an helmet of copper upon his head, and he was armed with a coat of mail; and the weight of the coat was five thousand shekels of copper. And he had greaves of copper upon his legs, and *kidon* of copper between his shoulders. And the staff of his spear was like a weaver's beam; and his spear's head weighed six hundred shekels of iron: and one bearing his shield went before him'. Also in I Samuel 21:9, Ahimelech the priest gives David the 'sword of Goliath the Philistine, whom thou slewest in the valley of Elah'. The second version is in II Samuel, 21:19 which describes duels fought by the warriors of David with Philistine warriors in the city of Gob, according to which Goliath was killed by Elhanan: '… Elhanan the son of Jaare-oregim, a Bethlehemite, slew … Goliath the Gittite, the staff of whose spear was like a weaver's beam'. The account that is given in I Chronicles 20:5 makes no mention of a duel between Goliath and David or Elhanan, but only says: '…and Elhanan, the son of Jair slew Lahmi the brother of Goliath the Gittite, whose spear staff was like a weaver's beam', as though Goliath himself was famous and well known to all.

The story was subjected to interpretations, and attempts were already made in ancient times to reconcile the contradictions between the versions. In the Septuagint of the 2nd century BCE (in Codex Vaticanus B version) Chapter 17 is shorter than the one in the traditional MT version, and some think it is a translation of an earlier text of the Bible (see below). Josephus (First century CE) relates the battle between David and Goliath in faithful accord with the description in I Samuel 17 (*Antiquities*, VI, 170-192). But later on in describing the duels between the warriors of David and those of the Philistines, he notes that Ἐφὰν Ephan (he means Elhanan), a relative of David, killed the bravest Philistine warrior (Ibid. 7:302). He does not mention the name 'Goliath', perhaps to avoid conflict with the story of David and Goliath. Rashi (11th century CE) states in his commentary that Elhanan is David, while in the commentary by Radak (12th-13th centuries CE), Elhanan kills the person who was *with* Goliath, presumably his brother Lahmi.

In modern research as well, the story arouses many disputes. There is a controversy about the degree of realism and fantasy in it. There is also no agreement as to the time it was written down. Some claim that this was close to the time the event occurred at the beginning of the monarchy period, while others postpone its writing to the end of the Judaean monarchy and even to Second Temple times. The scholars employ a variety of research methods such as textual analysis (literary and philological) of the story, historical analysis, and also a comparative analysis with archaeological findings. However, even if they rely on the same evidence, their interpretations are subjective and they reach different and contradictory conclusions. We present below the main views.

A.1. The story of the duel has no historical basis

Galling believes that the story of the duel is a 'legend'. He examined the armament of Goliath and deduced that it did not correspond with archaeological finds of the Mycenaean period nor with later periods. The Philistines portrayed on the Medinet Habu wall relief which describes the battle between the Sea Peoples who invaded Egypt and the army of Rameses III (1186-1154 BCE) are not wearing scale armor, helmets and greaves. Their weapons consist of a spear, thrusting sword, bow and arrow and a small shield (1965: 155). On one hand, scale armor was widespread in Mesopotamia, Syria and Egypt during the Bronze and Iron Age and is not typical of the Mycenaean or Greek world. The helmet of Goliath was of an Assyrian type, pointed, without protection for the forehead and nose. On the other hand, greaves were clearly used in the Greek world. This means that the story of David and Goliath was written in the 8th century at the earliest. The description of the weaponry is eclectic, from a variety of types and regions, and they reflect both the times of the writer and earlier times (Ibid. 165).

Garfinkel (with Ganor) exposed in Khirbet Qeiyafa a fortified city which he identified with Sha'arayim, which is mentioned in the story of the battle in the Elah Valley. In 2008 he discovered an ostracon with a Hebrew inscription in Proto-Canaanite script, and deduced that the Davidic kingdom has already existed by 1000 BCE. He attributes the destruction of the city, around 980 BCE, to one of the battles against the Philistines (Garfinkel 2013). However, Garfinkel doubts the veracity of the story because of two problems. Firstly, tradition ascribes the killing of Goliath to Elhanan ben Yaari. Secondly, at the end of the battle it is said: 'And David took the head of the Philistine, and brought it to Jerusalem ...' (I Samuel 17:54), but David conquered Jerusalem only when he became king. Garfinkel stresses the geographical significance of the story. Tradition chose to locate the battle in the Valley of Elah since this was the gateway to the Kingdom of Judah through which the Philistines penetrated in the direction of Hebron, Jerusalem and Lachish. Soldiers were stationed in the fortress of Sha'arayim, and to brace their spirits on the eve of battle the epic story of the duel was recited to them as a metaphor for the situation of the Kingdom of Judah – the weak against the strong, the few against the many (Garfinkel 2009).

A.2. The story was created and edited after David's period (8th century BCE till the Second Temple period)

Na'aman thinks that the version in II Samuel 21 is the original one, and that the version in I Samuel derives from it and replaces Elhanan with David. In his view, the fortress exposed in Sha'arayim did not belong to Judah but to the Kingdom of Gath which was at a distance of 11.5 km from it. He identifies it with the settlement Gob where, according to II Samuel 21:18-19 two other battles were fought between the warriors of David and the champion warriors of the Philistines who were called '*yelîdê hārāpā*'. Na'aman agrees with those who think that the name of the city 'Nob' in verse 16 should be read as 'Gob' where another confrontation occurred between Yishbi, a Philistine of the sons of the giant, and David who was assisted by Abishai the son of Zeruiah. According to this researcher, the source for all these stories were the chronicles written no later than the first half of the 8th century BCE which he calls 'The Chronicles of the Early Kings of Israel'. The later editor of the story in I Samuel also linked it with Gob, but changed the name of the place to Sha'arayim since that was name of the settlement in his time (2008: 2-7).

Zakovitz and Shinan reject the harmonization approach that identifies Elhanan with David and believe that the ascription of the victory to David is a relatively late variation of the victory of Elhanan over Goliath, the Philistine from Gath. Stories that were told about marginal characters were later on transferred to the central figure – David. Proof of this is that in addition to the story of Elhanan there are other anecdotes about single combats fought by the warriors of David, such as the combat in Nob with Yishbi whose weapons resemble those of Goliath, and with 'a man of great stature' who cursed the God of Israel as Goliath had done (I Chronicles 20: 4-8). Benaiah, chief of David's warriors, killed lion as David did, and like him went with only a staff in his hand to meet the Egyptian who was armed with a spear, and killed him with his own weapon (II Samuel 23: 20-21) (2004: 193-194).

Malamat indicates that a duel was like a contest between technological means, and the deceptive tactics of David which was merely an accessory to the 'technologically' inexpensive, rapid and long-rang means he had in hand – a sling and a stone. Their range was sometimes even longer than that of a bow and arrow. Military superiority was always given to the side that had weapons of a longer range. In his opinion the duel occurred at the beginning of the monarchy period, but the story was composed at a later date and contained 'a thick layer of religious ideology' (2007: 19).

Naveh thinks that the figure of Achish in the stories about David is anachronistic, and that his name is analogous to the name of Achish, King of Ekron in the 7th century BCE, whose dedication inscription was found during the excavations at Tell Miqne (biblical Ekron): 'This temple was built by 'Akish, the son of Padi, son of Ada, son of Ya'ir, ruler of Ekron, for Patgiah his (divine) lady. May she bless him, and guard him, and prolong his days, and bless his land'. The source of the name Achish is Aegean: Αχαιος, which means 'Achaian'. The name reflects a national Aegean revival among the Philistines of that period. In Assyrian documents, Achish the King of Ekron, is named 'Ikausu which is derived from Αχαιος. These documents also mention the King of Ashdod, called 'Iamani' which means 'Greek' in Assyrian (1998: 121).

Rofé found in the duel story an earlier structural pattern of a folk tale, and a second later one which was theological. The source of the story was in the popular folk tales from the days of David about the heroic exploits of the warriors in his court. At that time the practice of holding single combats was widespread. These stories were handed down from generation to generation and were eventually attributed to David himself (1986: 77). The considerable length of Chapter 17 is typical of the later writing. Rofé bases himself on a precise philological analysis which concludes that the story of the duel in its final form was composed only during Second Temple times, apparently at the end of the Persian period. The text includes plene spelling ('דוב', 'קליא'); late vocabulary ('יהושיע',

'רע לבבך', 'ויחתו ויראו', 'השכם והערב', 'ברו'); syntax that is similar to that of Chronicles composed in the 5th century BCE, which is even later that the Book of Deuteronomy composed in the 7th-6th centuries BCE; prepositions ('מעל ל-'); impersonal noun combinations with a personalized pronoun ('לחם הזה'); the use of the simple past tense and time indicating sentences instead of using the reversed past ('וכשוב' 'וכראות' instead of 'ויהי'). In addition, the term 'אִישׁ-הַבֵּנַיִם' (man of the space between) is found only in the Qumran scroll known by the name 'War of the Sons of Light against the Sons of Darkness'. Moreover, this is a translation of the military term 'το μεταιχμίον' (the space between rival camps) that appeared in Greek only in the 5th century BCE. Another Greek analogy with connections to the Iliad is the motif of the representative type of single combats such as the duel between Paris and Menelaus which comes instead of general war and decides the outcome of the battle. The story cannot reflect the realities of the period in which it was written, but only the literary influence of the Homeric epic. This is because Judah did not exist then as a state but only as a province of the Persian Empire. The Greek influence was possible since contacts between Judah and the Greek world had been created even before the conquest of Alexander the Great through merchants and Greek mercenaries, because Persia then controlled Asia Minor. So that even if the author did not know Greek and had not read the Iliad, he could have known about it orally (ibid. 77).

The story contains theological concepts and expressions of a late period, for example 'the living God' as opposed to dead gods. In David's speech '...the Lord of Hosts, the God of the armies of Israel' (I Samuel 17:45) emphasizes that God is not accompanied by the heavenly hosts that were reverenced in Judah during the 8th century BC under Assyrian influence, but by the army of Israel. The earliest appearance of 'the Lord of Hosts' is in the prayer of Hezekiah which was composed in the 6th century BCE (ibid. 81). The phrase '...for the battle is the Lord's' (I Samuel 17:47) parallels the one in II Chronicles 20:15: '...for the battle is not yours, but God's' (Ibid. 83). The final recension of the story corresponds to the period of eschatological expectations for national liberation as expressed in the Book of Nehemiah in which phrases can be found similar to those in I Samuel 17. Recensions of the 5th century were made also in the prophecies of the restoration of David as king and redeemer of Israel in the books of Hosea, Jeremiah and Ezekiel. In that period, under Persian influence, the belief in the resurrection of the dead became implanted in Jewish thought. David defeating Goliath embodied the redeemer and liberator from Persian rule (ibid. 88-89).

Finkelstein believes that the stories of David and the Philistines, even if the source for some of them is more ancient, belongs to the David and Solomon cycle of stories composed during the days of Josiah, King of Judah (640-609 BCE) (with Silbermn, 2003; with Silbermn, 2006). They express the 'Deut. approach'.[10] Their writing is biased and

---

[10] The outlook or Deut. spirit is named after the Book of Devarim (Duteronomy, also called 'מִשְׁנֵה תּוֹרָה' Mishne Torah – second low) which was translated into Greek as Δευτερονόμιον and in Latin as Deuteronomium. Most of the book is a speech by Moses reviewing the history of the people of Israel and the laws it received. The Book of Deuteronomy stresses the oneness of God and the centralization of the ritual cult 'in the place that God will choose', in the Temple. Also given stress is social justice. It is commonly accepted that the book should be identified with the one found in the Temple during the days of Josiah, who conducted in its spirit the cultic reforms he introduced in 622 BCE. The ideological and stylistic influence of Deuteronomy is also evident in

reflects the policy of Josiah in the struggle between Babylon and Egypt under the 26th Saite dynasty (2006: 181-184). The description of Goliath derives from two sources of inspiration: from the reality of Greek mercenaries who were then the dominant component in the Egyptian army, and from narrative literature – the Homeric epic. Finkelstein presents a number of proofs that the story was of a later date:

- The Philistines were included among the Sea Peoples described on the wall reliefs of the temple of Rameses III (1186-1154 BCE) in Medinet Habu in Egypt. But their weapons are different from those of Goliath. They do not have heavy armor, a bronze helmet and greaves, and use a single spear. Although armament items similar to his can be found in the Aegean world from the Mycenaean to the Classical period, helmets and greaves made of metal were relatively rare until the 7th century BCE. The armament of Goliath was typical of Greek hoplites, ordinary Greek soldiers carrying heavy armor, thousands of them serving as mercenaries in the Saite army, and they were the source for the biblical description of Goliath. The hoplites also served as an Egyptian stationary force to control the country at the end of the 7th century BCE. This can be derived from Aegean pottery found in the fort of Mesad Hashavyahu in Judah and from an inscription in the citadel of Arad that mentions 'Kittim' mercenaries (from Kition in Cyprus). Contrary to his view, Naveh and Aharoni believe that these mercenaries served the Kings of Judah (Naveh 1992: 557-558; Aharoni 1981: 12-13). Finkelstein is aware of three difficulties in his proposal. The first is that the Greek hoplites usually wore armor made of bronze plates and not scale armor which was typical of the East. The second was that shield bearers, as far as he knew, were not mentioned in Greek texts or depicted on vases of the 7th to 5th centuries BCE. They are only portrayed on Assyrian reliefs shielding the archers. He has two explanations for this: either the biblical author inserted Assyrian elements into his description, or the Greek hoplites during their service in the East wore scale armor and were assisted by shield bearers. Armor scales were found in Mesad Hashavyahu in Judah where the Greek mercenaries were stationed, as well as in Tell Daphnae (biblical Tahpanhes) in Egypt where mercenaries were also quartered (2002: 145-146). Thirdly – the hoplite helmets protected the forehead, and it is improbable that David struck exactly on the forehead of Goliath. He rejects the supposition that David struck Goliath's knee (Deem 1978: 251-349), and assumes that this was a literary invention meant to glorify David (ibid. 146, n. 25). See below for my suggestion to solve the difficulties in Sections C. 3: 2-4.
- The 'Cherethites and the Pelethites', the foreign mercenaries of David belong to the 7th century BCE. In Egyptian sources they are not mentioned among the Sea

---

the prophecies of Jeremiah. The outlook and style resembling the Book of Deuteronomy are also clearly seen in the editing of the books of the early prophets: Joshua and Judges, Samuel and Kings. From this scholars have inferred since Noth the existence of a Deut. school of thought that was active since 622 BCE until the time of the Babylonian Exile and that edited and emended the books of the early prophets. Some scholars date it back to the reign of Hezekiah who also aspired to centralize the cult in Jerusalem and eradicated the idols. There are many and varied approaches that extend the writing or editing of the early prophets to the Second Temple period, from the Return to Zion until the Hellenistic and Roman periods. According to the Deut. outlook, the reforms of Hezekiah and Josiah were insufficient to prevent the destruction decreed on both kingdoms because of the sins of Jereboam who established the cult of Asherah in Bethel, and the sins of Manasseh, who introduced it into the Temple (I Kings 13: 2; II Kings 23: 15-16). The reforms only postponed the final destiny.

Peoples. Cretan (Cherethite) mercenaries reached out region only from the 7th century BCE onwards, while the name 'Pelethites', as William Albright noted, stems from the Greek term *peltastai*: regular soldiers lightly armed whose name derived from *pelta*, the light shield they bore. They appear on vase paintings from the 6th century BCE, but were mentioned for the first time by Thucydides in the 5th century BCE (2006: 270- 271). It is not reasonable to suppose that indigent Judah of the days of David could afford mercenaries, and the aim of the later editor was to glorify him as a strong and rich king. Another reason was to give legitimacy to the cooperation of the kings of Judah after Joshiah with Egypt and the Greek mercenaries (2002: 149-150).
- Philological analysis shows that the stories of David and the Philistines are of a later date, since the term 'seren' is mentioned in them. The source of this term is Greek, from the word *tyrannos* (evolved from the Anatolian *tarwanis*), which appeared only in the 7th century BCE in Western Asia Minor (2006: 269-270). In addition, literary expressions such as 'until this very day' is typical of Deut. writings (ibid. 178).
- The spirit of the composition is Deut.: The aim of the battle is the victory of God, 'for the battle is the Lord's' (I Samuel 17:47). We do not find this in the story of Elhanan and Goliath, and this implies it is earlier than the story of David and Goliath (ibid. 180-181).
- In the story about David in the service of Achish, King of Gath, settlements are mentioned which existed only towards the end of the monarchy period, specifically in the period of Josiah: ʿAroʿer, Ramat Hanegev, Yattir (ibid. 179).
- Alliances among Philistine cities were typical of the federations in the Aegean world during the Archaic period (750-480 BCE), but not in the Ancient East.

Finkelstein deduces from all this that the figures appearing in the stories about David correspond to personalities in the days of Josiah. David is to Josiah as Achish, King of Gath is to Achish, King of Ekron. The positive description of Achish was meant to give legitimacy to the economic cooperation of Josiah with him (ibid. 176-178). Goliath was armed like a Greek hoplite in the army of Egyptian Pharaoh Necho II (610-595 BCE) who was the enemy of Josiah and killed him in Megiddo. The story of the duel was composed in the days preceding the confrontation between them. There is some analogy between the name 'Goliath' and 'Elyattes', the tyrant of Lydia (610-560 BCE) who hired out the hoplites to Egypt (ibid. 280, n. 33). The story of the duel was created at the end of the 7th century BCE with a background of increasing tensions between Judah and Egypt, and ahead of the clash between two national dreams. The dream of Judah was to reestablish the united kingdom of David and Solomon, and the dream of Egypt was to reestablish her empire in the Near East. Egypt had already taken control over a large part of Philistia. The inhabitants of Judah were well aware of the threatening Greek presence and understood the message conveyed by the story, that Josiah would defeat the elite Greek troops in the Egyptian army just as David had overcome the apparently unconquerable Goliath (ibid. 182-184). In 609 BCE Josiah went out against Necho who was conducting a military campaign against Babylon, and was killed by him at Megiddo (II Kings 23:29). The death of Josiah shattered all the hopes of the Deut. circles in purifying the cult and in national empowerment. The marks of this traumatic encounter with the Greek-Saitic hoplites in

Megiddo remained in recorded memory for generations, and features in the messianic speculations of Judaism and Christianity (ibid. 190-191).

However, even if true that Goliath was armed like a hoplite, then there are difficulties with some claims made by Finkelstein. If the story of Achish was meant to justify economic cooperation with the Philistine cities, it is not reasonable that Goliath the Philistine should be represented as the ultimate adversary of God, Israel and David. In the same way, if the story of the Cherethites and the Pelethites was meant to give legitimacy to the cooperation with the Saites and their mercenaries – why then to portray hostile Goliath as a Saitic hoplite? More than that: according to Deut. historiography, the alliance that Judah made with Egypt against Babylon was what brought about her destruction. The prophets Jeremiah and Ezekiel abhor the Saites and their mercenaries as the enemies of God, and describe their annihilation by divine fiat. See my proposals to resolve the issue in Sections E, F.

Yadin thinks that Chapter 17 reflects the Philistines and Jewish people of the 6th century BCE, and not of the 11th century BCE. It is an accepted assumption that the final recension of Deut. historiography is post-586 BCE, and it is not likely that all the details of the story remained unmodified. However, it should not be considered a fable invented by the biblical writer who worked within a Jewish milieu, particularly because of its salient Aegean components, such as military prowess to give legitimacy to the future king; the μονομαχία, contest of champions, as determining the fate of war; The arms that Goliath bore; and the concept of 'אִישׁ־הַבֵּנַיִם' (man of the in-between space) which is borrowed from the concept of 'το μεταίχμιον' (2004: 378-381). Moreover, Yadin claims that the question whether a duel actually took place should not be asked since it was a 'collective memory', a dialogue between the past and present, an attempt to reconstruct and revive the past so as to cope better with the rising hegemony of Greek culture (ibid. 386). The story should be read with the Iliad as its inter-text. Unlike the descriptions of war in the Book of Judges, it has a lot of parallels with Homer (the two camps; the challenge to a duel; the hanging of the bodies of Saul and his sons on the walls of the city), and also contrasts (the handsome lad without arms is a Homeric anti-hero; David discards the armor of Saul as opposed to Patroclus who wears the armor of Achilles) (ibid. 389-391). Additionally, in the description of Goliath attention is given to minute details just as in the Homeric epic, which is not typical of the restrained style of biblical description. According to Yadin, the biblical narrator use Homeric content and style because the Deut. historiography, which is the national epic of the consolidation of Israel out of a loose alliance of the tribes into a nation and state by David, was composed in the period in which Pan-Hellenic identity was also being consolidated. In the Greek world the local, ethnic identities were constructed on the basis of a renaissance of the past, the cult of heroes and their tombs as a means for affiliation with it and also resulted from the spread of the Homeric epic in the 7th century BCE in the Eastern Mediterranean. For example, a tomb was constructed in Salamis in Cyprus on the Homeric model (Karageorgis 1995: 9-12). Among the Philistines, who were aware of their kinship with the Greeks in Cyprus, national revival was also occurring at that time. From the inscription of 'Akyš the son of Padi and the seal of Ddymš the son of 'Lykm it appears that the Semitic names of earlier generations were discarded for Greek names. In the Bible, the Philistines are perceived as 'national other' and are termed the 'uncircumcised'. In the Septuagint the word 'פלשתי' is translated as αλλόφυλος (foreign, a member of another tribe). Goliath is the archetypical Philistine. The story of David and Goliath is part of the national narrative of the ascendancy of the greatest Israelite king. In order to forge it, the Bible recruits the national narrative of the rival collective, and through a polemical dialogue with it, undermines its claims and thus confirms the superiority of Israel over Greece. This was also a competition between the national epics of rivals and the poetic sensibilities inherent in them. The biblical narrator conduct polemical debate on two fronts. The first, by distorting the conventions of the Greek epic – the mighty hero, the professional warrior, impeccably armed, is defeated by an unarmed handsome lad. The second, by subtle struggle against its style – in his description of Goliath and his weaponry, the biblical narrator adopts for a moment the Homeric style. David, who rejects this Greek 'equipment', rejects not only Greek military ideals but also the literary ones. He chooses simple tools, just as the Bible style does. Just as David, in answering the challenge of Goliath, fights according to his own monomachist conditions and defeats him with his own weapons, so does the biblical narrative in Chapter 17 adopt the Homeric style which is foreign to him. The light and agile fighter defeats the heavy and slow one. At the end of the confrontation the elaborate style is discarded, and Goliath dies in a simple, pellucid verse of biblical prose (ibid. 394-395).

Heard opposes Yadin by asking how Deut. historiography could be defined as a 'national epic' when it ends with the destruction and exile of the Kingdom of Judah and the captivity of its king. Moreover, why should a 'national epic' be composed in the 6th or 5th century BCE through 'polemical debate' with Greek culture? In his view, Deut. historiography in the 6th and 5th centuries dealt with the definition of the status of Judah (and of Israel before it) vis-à-vis the Mesopotamian powers, and to a lesser degree, with the Egyptian one. There does not seem to be any reference in it to the Hellenic invaders (2006).

Fantalkin, like Finkelstein, identifies the heroes of the duel with Josiah and the Aegean-Saitic hoplite. He dates the story to the end of the 7th century BCE, before and in expectation of the confrontation between Josiah and Pharaoh Necho. The 'Cherethites and the Pelethites' of David reflect Carian mercenaries in the service of the Saite rule in Judah (2008: 350-368, 430). In his study he shows that there exists a correspondence between the dates of the appearance and disappearance of Eastern Greek pottery at various sites in the country at the end of the 7th century and the period of the Egyptian conquest (2008: 280-285). He concludes from this that: 'Although the Aegean mercenaries appeared in our region for a short period of time, the encounter was traumatic for the Kingdom of Judah' (ibid. 383-384). He sums up by saying: 'The description of the duel between David and Goliath by the Deut. historian is merely the transmission of a complex allegorical message before the approaching confrontation between the Kingdom of Judah and the Saite dynasty represented among others by mercenaries of a Greek origin' (ibid. 430).

With regard to the term 'אִישׁ-הַבֵּנַיִם', Fantalkin negates the reference to 'το μεταίχμιον' as its origin. This is because in Greek there is no term for 'μεταίχμιον people' fighting within this space, and because it does not appear in texts written before Herodotus (VI.112.1; VIII.140B.3). In his opinion, the Deut. author visualized a phalanx formation in front of which marched fighters called πρόμαχοι as they are also described in the Iliad. Goliath stood between two fighters on either side of him, and this was the source for his epithet (ibid. 343-346). Regarding the way in which Goliath was armed, Fantalkin suggests new interpretations for the words 'צִנָּה' tsina and 'כִּידוֹן' kidon. 'נֹשֵׂא הַצִּנָּה' nose hatsina is really the one who carries the arms, and not shield bearer. This is based on the Septuagint in which the translation for צִנָּה is τα ὅπλα. This is the plural form of a direct object, which in Fantalkin's view is not derived from the word ὅπλον (singular) in its first sense as a shield, but in its second sense as a weapon (ibid. 337-338). The כִּידוֹן that Goliath carried 'between his shoulders' is not a javelin or a kind of sword but a shield (ibid. 333, 347-348). Fantalkin is aware of the disparity between his suggesting and the standard hoplite armaments during the period of Josiah, since carrying a shield on the back conforms to an earlier stage in hoplite warfare. But he claims that it is just such imprecise elements that indicate the veracity of the story, which is faithful to a situation in which the final form of this type of warfare had not yet been consolidated, and was more in conformity with the end of the 7th century BCE (ibid. 348-350).

In my opinion, one cannot ignore the fact that the word צִנָּה in all its various instances and variations in the Bible has the meaning of a shielding and protecting device and not a weapon of attack.[11] It is, however, reasonable to suppose that Goliath's shield bearer *also* carried some reserve weapons, which is why they were included in the Septuagint as τα ὅπλα. The hoplite acquired his name not from his shield but from the ὅπλα which was a combination of weapons and protective devices that he held in his hands and carried on his body (Krentz 2007: 69). The hoplite shield was usually called an 'aspis' ασπίς and every hoplite had a ὑπασπιστής, a shield bearer who bore his heavy shield until the moment when the battle began (see below, Section C.3.3). The heavy weight of the shield made this the first item to be cast away when the warrior had to flee for his life, as did poet-warriors such as Archilochus (Diehl, Frg. 51), Alcaeus (Herodotus V.95), and Anacreon (Diehl, Frg. 6). Spartan mothers would adjure their sons going out to battle, saying that they should return 'Ἢ ταν ἢ επί τας' - with it or on it (Plutarch, *Moralia, Lacaenarum Apophthegmata* 6.16). Until the 7th century the *aspis* was carried by a grip in its center for the palm of the hand, and it could also be hung with a strap over the back for protection while retreating. This back strap was not attached to the hoplite shield, which was carried by a grip in its center to the arm and by a tether for the palm near its edge. The back remained exposed, and this was the reason for the scorn that Tyrtaeus

---

[11] 'But let all those that put their trust in thee rejoice: let them even shout for joy, because thou defendest them: let them also that lover thy name be joyful in thee. For thou, Lord, wilt bless the righteous; with favor wilt thou compass him as with a shield' (Psalms 5: 12-13). 'He that dwelleth in the secret place of the most High shall abide under the shadow of the Almighty. I will say of the Lord, He is my refuge and my fortress: my God; in him will I trust. Surely he shall deliver thee from the snare of the fowler, and from the noisome pestilence. He shall cover thee with his feathers, and under his wings shalt thou trust: his truth shall be thy shield and buckler. Thou shalt not be afraid for the terror by night; nor for the arrow that flieth by day. Nor for the pestilence that walketh in darkness; nor for the destruction that wasteth at noonday. A thousand shall fall at thy side, and ten thousand at thy right hand; but it shall not come nigh thee' (Psalms 91: 1-7).The Bible also compares the weight of the shield and buckler. In I Kings 10: 16-17 it is said: 'And king Solomon made two hundred targets of beaten gold; six hundred shekels of gold went to one target. And he made three hundred shields of beaten gold: three pounds of gold went to one shield'. This means that the shield weighed about 150 or 180 shekels. In a parallel version in II Chronicles 9: 15-16 it says: 'And king Solomon made two hundred targets of beaten gold: six hundred shekels of beaten gold went to one target. And three hundred shields made he of beaten gold: three hundred shekels of gold went to one shield'. The implication is that the צִנָּה (heavy shield) was twice the weight of the light shield; and there is no point in comparing the weight of an assault weapon with the weight of a shield.

showed when he wrote in 640-630 BCE to those warriors who had been injured in their backs – meaning that they fled the battlefield (Tyrtaeus, CURFRAG.tlg-0.266-7). The *aspis* was very concave in order to improve its protection and so that it could be rested on the shoulder, which is why it was called κοίλης hollow (Alcaeus Frg. 140, 1-10. Tyrtaeus, Frg. 19: 'κοίληις ασπίσι φραξάμ[ενοι'). It was therefore not comfortable to bear it on the back. In most descriptions of the hoplites in literature and the visual arts they do not carry shields on their backs. Like Goliath, the hoplites carried swords or javelins behind them over their shoulders. Some scholars interpret the word כִּידוֹן which is rare in the Bible, as a sword. This explains, in their view, why it was absent in the description of Goliath, but is mentioned in v. 51: 'Therefore David ran, and stood upon the Philistine, and took his sword, and drew it out of the sheath thereof, and slew him, and cut off his head therewith'. Some believe that this was a long straight sword, while others think it was wide and curved of the type called scimitar, or that it was a sickle sword (see the references in Garsiel 1997). In any case, this assumption contradicts what is said in v. 45: 'Then said David to the Philistine, Thou comest to me with a sword and spear, and with a shield'. Thus Goliath carried three kinds of arms that differed in their use and size. A different source and interpretation may be suggested for כִּידוֹן. It may have been derived from the Greek word εγ-χειριδίος – 'within the palm of the hand' - which appears in Aeschylus (6th-5th century BCE), and in Herodotus the word εγχειρίδιον means dagger (Liddell & Scott 1985: 223). In transference to the Hebrew the εγ was deleted, and what remained was the χεῖ (כִי) at the beginning of the word כִּירִידיוֹן which therefore received the 'dagesh' (strong stress) for the first consonant – כ.[12] A similar path was taken in the opposite direction with the Semitic word כְּתֹנֶת ('ktonet') which the Greeks adopted and changed into χιτών. Here the stressed כ was replaced by the unstressed Greek χεῖ. In the Bible, other Greek words from the military sphere were adopted (see below, Sections C.5 and D).

A.3. The story was written around the time of David

Zinger rejects the late dating of Finkelstein and the identification of Goliath with an armed hoplite in the Saite army for a number of reasons. The description of Goliath is of an eclectic nature that draws upon various sources from different periods of time. The duel of champions is a typical folk tale of bravery that was meant to glorify David. The original story may have been that of Elhanan the Bethlehemite which was 'stolen' and added to the exploits of David with significant additions. Championship duels between individuals were widespread in the Ancient East and in Greece, and especially typical of early combat traditions, while the phalanx, hoplite warfare in battle formation teams began to take shape only during the time of Homer. In addition, a series of studies have proved the reliability and precision of oral traditions over the centuries through which survive the memories of battles, the identity of the rivals, the arena of the events that took place, and the general course of the struggle. (The Achaean-Mycenaean coalition the Homer describes corresponds to the Ahhiyawa of the Hittite Empire period while in

---

[12] On the other hand, there is a probability that the source for 'כִּידוֹן' (kidon) is Akkadian. Ben Yosef Tawil notes that in the Akkadian documents from Allah, Nuzi and Amar the word 'kattinu' is mentioned which refers to an object or decoration made of copper with embedded stones or a metal weapon (2010: 161). Heltzer says that 'kattinu' is etymologically and semantically equivalent to the 'kidon', and means a sickle-sword (1989: 65-68).

Homer's days Troy and Mycenae were isolated villages). This is valid also for the biblical story of the struggle between Israel and the Philistines at the beginning of the monarchy period (2006: 77-82).

However, we know of many instances of the use of champion combat in all periods of time, as a solution to continual battles or territorial disputes. Sometimes the victors used these combats to pave the way to the throne. A famous ascendancy story is told about Darius III, King of Persia (336-330 BCE). His predecessor Artaxerxes III (358-338 BCE) went out to battle against the Kadusi tribe (Καδούσιοι) who were known throughout ancient times as excelling in infantry warfare (Justin 10.3; Diodorus 17.6.1-2. Strabo XI.13). Their champion provoked the Persian fighters and challenged them to a duel, and only Darius dared to go out against him and defeated him. The king showered him with expensive gifts and he was called the bravest of all the Persians. For this reason he was considered suitable for kingship after the powerful vizier Bagoas eliminated the king, his son Artaxerxes IV and all the royal family. Later on Bagoas was killed by order of Darius who was afraid of him (this is what happened to Avner, the general of Saul's army, who helped David to gain the throne as was eliminated later on). On another similar duel between Pittacus of Mytilene and Phrynon the Athenian, see below, Section C.4. It is also accepted today by scholars that in Homeric description as well as in mass hoplite warfare, even if the soldiers came to the battlefield in an orderly phalanx formation[13] they also developed into free warfare formations. We cannot even infer from the elegies of Tyrtaeus of the mid-7th century BCE describing the formation of soldiers in close ranks standing firm and shielding each other, that he is depicting warfare in phalanxes as in the classical period, but that he is merely stresses its advantage as compared with disorderly retreat under pressure of the enemy and the desertion of comrades in arms (Van Wees 1994:142). Snodgrass noted that most of the vase paintings in the first half of the 7th century BCE described duels between individuals and not mass warfare (2006: 314-315). Peter Krentz pointed out that although hoplites in ancient times were deployed in massed formation, they fought as individuals against other individuals or in small groups. The paintings on the aryballos in Paris and the aryballos in Syracuse truly represent this fighting (2007: 76-77, ill. 8-9).

---

[13] The phalanx formation consisted of close ranks of hoplite fighters wearing heavy armor, helmets and greaves. Their standard equipment was δόρυ, a long sharp spear held in the right hand, about 2-3m long with a wooden shaft and an iron blade, which served both for spearing and for throwing. In the left hand they held the *aspis*, a large round shield, by means of an arm strap in its center and a palm grip at its edge. This shield also protected the warrior on the left. The sword was a supplementary weapon used for face to face combat. The phalanx formation was meant to push back and penetrate the ranks of the enemy, and the victory was decided when these ranks collapsed. Philip II, King of Macedonia (359-336 BCE) is credited with the invention of the σάρισα sarisa which came up to 6m in length. Because of their heavy weight the warriors held them in both hands. The *aspis* was replaced by the small shield – the *peltha* - which was hung by a strap from the neck and covered the left shoulder, in which there was also an arm grip. In the Macedonian phalanx the number of ranks was double that of the classical Greek phalanx and increased from 8-10 rows to 16-32. There is a debate over which of the two was earlier and what caused what. Did the development of hoplite arms cause the development of the phalanx tactic in warfare, or the contrary? It is not of interest here to go into this in depth. But see Snodgrass (2006) on the gradual development of the 'hoplite reform'. An additional debate exists on the form of warfare in the Iliad. Was this mass fighting (as, for example, Latacz believes) or in free formations and duels. From the arms and armor Van Wees concludes that each warrior was armed according to his own preference in warfare. For example, Paris and Teukros (Teucer) were skilled archers. While Paris wore only a leopard skin, Teucer, although he possessed a helmet and shield, fought without them (Van Wees 1994: 131).

Garsiel (2007, 2008) claims that the story is early. 'אִישׁ-הַבֵּנַיִם' is not a late military term but a play on words by the author such as 'Goliath of Gath'. Elhanan is the one who killed Goliath. Since he was loved by many they began to call him David from the word 'dod', which in Hebrew means 'beloved', while name 'יַעְרֵי אֹרְגִים' Jaäre-orgim is a corruption of the word 'יִשַׁי' Yishai (as suggested by Honeyman 1948). Goliath was a fearful giant with exceptional metal-based arms (Garsiel 2008: 59-60). Garsiel finds weak points in the claims of those in favor of a late date:

- From a linguistic consideration, if there really was some Greek influence on our story, why was there no recognizable influence of Greek words on the Book of Samuel in general and on this story in particular? For the sake of comparison, there is a very clear influence of Greek and Roman words on the vocabulary of rabbinical narratives. Against this, I shall later on show that there do exist Greek words in the Bible from a specific field.
- The arms mentioned in the story of the duel resemble those in the Homeric narrative not because it was influenced by it, but because both stories describe ancient warriors, the Mycenaeans and the Philistines of Aegean origins. Metal helmets of the third millennium were found in excavations, and scale armor of the Late Bronze Age. Indeed, they were rare and therefore only a small group of Philistine giants ('the sons of the giant') were equipped with them in the 11th or at the beginning of the 10th century BCE. The arms of Goliath aroused amazement and paralysis among the Israelites because of its rarity, since they would not have been terrified at standard hoplite weaponry commonly seen among the mercenaries in Judah during the 7th century BCE (ibid. 69-70). As against this, the late editor described the state and reaction of the *early* Israelites without such weapons, and not the Israelites of his own day.
- Epic works were preserved for centuries through the technique of versions, accents, rhythm, cycle structure and mimicry. Information about the Mycenaean period was memorialized also in works of art such as the frescos in Akrotiri, vase paintings, etc. Against this, even if an early historical core story was preserved, one cannot assume that it passed down from generation to generation without editorial variations.
- Finkelstein and Silberman claim that the Deut. narrative praised David in order to glorify Josiah - but the Book of Samuel contains harsh criticism of David (the story of Bathsheba and Uriah). Against this, it is clear that the trend of the book was not to present a perfect superhuman ruler but rather his weakness as a man before God, who was the sole victor.
- The relations between the Philistines and Israel in the Book of Samuel were complex, with ups and downs, and therefore they cannot be regarded as bitter enemies during the reign of Josiah. Against this, the Philistines were the main rival of Israel in the territorial struggle over the country during the period of the Judges and the united monarchy. Even Uzziah and Hezekiah, Kings of Judah, fought against the Philistines (II Chronicles 26:6; II Kings 18:8). Moreover, their cults were regarded as dangerous competition for the religion of Israel, as in the prohibition to 'practice divination like the Philistines' (Isaiah 2:6), the death of Ahaziah, King of Israel because he consulted Baalzebub the god of Ekron (II

Kings 1:2), and the Jewish believers in Dagon during days of Josiah, according to the prophet Zephaniah (1:9). Beyond this, the figure of Goliath may not only have represented the Philistines in the period of Josiah, but other enemies of that time who were also of Aegean origin.

- Garsiel examines the challenge of Goliath and the panic of Saul and his army. Why did Saul not send fighters to eliminate Goliath? And if he did not find a candidate, why did he refuse the offer? Why was he struck with paralysis? Why did Goliath curse the God of the hosts of Israel? Garsiel believes that the duel was not representative championship combat meant to save human lives, as Yadin claims, but was meant to expose the intention of the gods, to foretell the outcome of the battle and to prevent unnecessary bloodshed. Many of the people of that region in ancient times believe that the gods were involved and took sides in wars. Therefore they asked their advice whether to go out to battle or not. Saul was in a quandary, and sent David into battle because he had proved that God had been with him in the past. In opposition to Garsiel, the question is why were all battles not conducted as 'prophesying duels' in order to prevent the shedding of blood? And what was the difference between a battle and a representative championship combat if in any case the sides attributed their victory or defeat to the gods?

According to Garsiel, the main thesis in the Book of Samuel is that God is the real power that acts behind the scenes. The kingdom of heaven is preferable to the kingdom of flesh and blood, and a rule that is established by divine anointment is better than the best of rulers. The book was composed by a circle of prophets who were active at the end of David's reign and during that of Solomon and underwent very little Deut. recension (ibid. 76-81). However, this thesis could also be suited to the days of the Second Temple before the Hasmoneans came to power, when there was no monarchy and only the rule of priests and scribes. There was expectation of a king who would be a descendant of David, but he would be the messiah, the messenger of God.

Maier who is excavating Tell es-Safi, the biblical Gath, discovered an *ostracon* of the 10th or 9th century BCE with letters in a Semitic script: אלות.וולת. At first he saw it as close to the name Goliath and a proof of the veracity and early origins of the story. He also estimated that the *ostracon* represented the Lydian name 'Elyattes' which, following Albright 1975: 513, was considered by many to be parallel etymologically to 'Goliath'. But in an article written in 2008 he negated this because of the absence of the initial 'gimel' and because the Y/υ (upsilon) in the name 'Elyattes' was pronounced in that period as the English 'u' and not as a 'y'. Therefore no direct link exists between the names on the *ostracon* and the name 'Goliath'. He now supports the suggestion made by H. C. Melchert that 'Goliath' originates from the personal Carian name 'w/uliat' which translates into Greek as Oliatos or Alaolos. It derives from the word walliwalli in Hittite, which means 'strong' (2008: 57-58). The problem is that this provides no solution to the absence of an initial 'gimel'.

Yasur-Landau indicates that Aegean motifs in all spheres of life had appeared in Philistia from the beginning of the Iron Age. In his opinion, the introduction of the word *seranim* which originates from Luwian was possible only in the period in which the rulers of

Philistia were non-local and their culture was not indigent, and had brought with them a foreign style of government and their own terminology. This means that it was only during the time when the Sea Peoples were migrating in the 12th century BCE, and not in the 7th century BCE when the Book of Judges and I Samuel were written, since at that time no foreign rulers had yet arrived in Philistia. In the stories of David in I Samuel 21-29, in addition to 'seranim' there are alternatives such as sarim 'שָׂרִים' and melekh 'מֶלֶךְ' which in the view of this researcher are local and much later in date. In the Ekron inscription, Aclhish calls himself 'שַׂר', and this conforms to the fact that all the rulers of Philistia in the 8th and 7th centuries BCE who are listed in Assyrian documents (except for Achish) have Semitic names (2010: 312-313, 343). Yasur-Landau accepts the usual identification of the goddess Ptgyh (for whom the 'Achaean' built a temple) with the Aegean goddess Ptgyh from πυθο-Γαια 'Gaia from Pytho' (the name of the Apolline oracle in Delphi) or Ποτ[ν[ια-Γαια (the lady Gaia) from the Greek word γη – which means earth. In his view, they guarded her cult in Philistia from the time of their migration in the 12th century BCE (ibid. 306).

Ben-Shlomo investigated Philistine iconography from the various archaeological finds I all the cities of Philistia during the Iron Age I and II periods (1200-586 BCE), and found that they were unique in all the southern Levant in their Aegean style traditions. Gradually, local influences were absorbed and a typical Philistine style was developed that included a merging of Aegean, Cypriot, Canaanite and Egyptian elements. Prominent Aegean motifs were the figures of women standing or sitting, the bird, and marine symbols such as fish and wave spirals. The Aegean and Cypriot motifs were dominant in the domestic sphere and in public places such as temples the dominant motifs were Canaanite (lion, bull, date palm). Further research shows that the migrants had a tendency to preserve their affiliations with their homeland in the domestic sphere (2010: 183-195). The Philistia pantheon included a mixture of Aegean and local gods. An Assyrian relief describes the bearing of statues of gods from conquered Gaza to Assyria such as the storm god of the Levantine type, two goddesses which are probably Aegean, sitting on chairs, one holding a kylix or flower, and the other a ring (ibid. 98-99).

To sum up the Philistine and Israelite relationships, they conducted territorial struggle from the time of their settlement in Canaan until the conquest of the cities of Philistia by Nebuchadnezzar and the exile of their inhabitants to Babylon at the end of the 7th century BCE. The constant friction sometimes engendered attempts at closer relations and temporary alliances against common enemies. In Judah, certain influences were made by the religion of Philistia such as consulting the oracle of Baalzebub and avoid stepping on the threshold like the Dagon worshippers. The Philistines on their part adopted the Canaanite language, and even their gods were given Semitic names such as Dagon, Ashtaroth, and Baalzebub. From a dedication inscription of the 7th century BCE found in Tell Miqne (biblical Ekron), they are shown worshipping Asherah, the Canaanite goddess of earth and fertility (Cogan & Gittin 1999). Yet at the same time they safeguarded their Aegean affiliations. This was given greater emphasis with the developments that began in the 8th century BCE in the Greek world. This duality is reflected in the dedication inscription of Achish. On one hand it is written according to the West Semitic tradition in language and spelling close to the Phoenician and in script close to the Hebrew. In it Achish gives details of his descent from the long dynastic line of Ekron rulers with Semitic names. On the other hand, his very name shows a revived emphasis on his Greek origins. He is also the first to initiate the building of a temple to Ptgyh. We have no other evidence of her cult. It may have been preserved from time of the Sea Peoples, or it also appeared or was restored in the 7th century BCE with the revival of Aegean culture. During that period the Pythian oracle played a central role in the Greek world and in the Greek settlement movement. In Ashdod at the end of the 8th century BCE a stranger mounted the throne who had been crowned by the citizens after they had deposed King Azuri. In an inscription of Sargon II he is called 'Iamani' which means he was of Ionic origins. All this shows that the elite stratum of Philistia society in the 7th century BCE absorbed people, ideas and cults from the Aegean world.

According to the Bible, Josiah at that time eradicated the cult of Asherah from Judah and Samaria after the discovery of the ancient Book of the Law in the Temple: 'And he brought out the grove [of Asherah] from the house of the Lord,… and burned it at the brook Kidron'. And in Bethel: '…he burned the high place, and stamped it small to powder, and burned the grove [of Asherah]' (II Kings 23: 6-15). The prophet Zephaniah also predicted the domination of Judah over Philistia: 'Woe unto the inhabitants of the sea coast, the nation of the Cherethites! The word of the Lord is against you; O Canaan, the land of the Philistines, I will even destroy thee, that there shall be no inhabitant …. And the coast shall be for the remnant of the house of Judah, they shall feed thereupon' (Zephaniah 2: 5-7). The territorial struggle was accompanied and sharpened the return to cultural and religious roots at the initiative of the rulers both in Philistia and in Judah.

B. Who were the opponents in the duel and when did the event take place?

At the extremity of the range of views the duel was perceived as a fiction, and opposed to it the view that it had occurred at the beginning of the monarchy period. But even the scholars of the latter school of thought agree that the history of the judges and monarchy period underwent some kind of editing. Naveh, Finkelstein, Rofé, and Yadin are convinced about the late accretions to the story. Even if a real core event occurred during the days of David, it was transmitted from one generation to another and passed through several editing processes. Today most researchers of the Bible agree that the process of editing of the books of Joshua, Judges, Samuel and Kings, although they include early sources, extended to the days of the Second Temple.[14]

But if the story reflects a polemical debate between national narratives and literary works, as Yadin believes, it is still necessary to examine what historical truth it may contain. In view of the strictures of Heard, we have to clarify the following. Firstly, who was the rival in the debate? Was Goliath really a Philistine of the early monarchy period or of the period of Josiah, or perhaps he was a symbol for another rival in the time of the Deut. author? Secondly, what was the counter-narrative, and how could a national epic end in defeat?

There are two issues that, if clarified, would in my opinion solve the overlaps and contradictions of the biblical versions. The first is: Why were the armor and weapons of Goliath given such prominence and importance in the story? The second is the name of the Philistine hero. This is one of the few names in the Bible that one cannot determine its meaning or significance. The earliest translators and commentators of the Bible tried to interpret it, but did so in a tendentious and expository manner, and on the assumption that the name was Hebrew. According to Rabbi Yohanan (180-280 CE): 'Goliath – Rabbi Yohanan said: because he stood barefaced ('glui panim') before God, as it says (I Samuel 17) 'choose you a man for you and let him come down to me' and the word 'man' only means God, as it says (Exodus 15) 'God is a man of war'. God said: I shall make him fall by the hand of a son of man, as it says (I Samuel 17) 'Now David was the son of a man of aristocracy...' (Babylonian Talmud, Tractate 'Sotah', 42b). Perhaps it will be helpful to understand the name of the other dominant Philistine in the stories about David, Achish. Whether he was really the King of Gath in the 10th century BCE or the King of Ekron in the 7th century BCE – his name in Greek means 'Achaean'.[15]

---

[14] From the school of thought that believes in the late recension of the Bible we should accept the view of the knowledge and influence of Greek narratives in the Bible (see my conclusions below). However, we should reject the opinion that attributes it entirely to the Hellenistic period.

[15] 'Achaeans' is the common term for Greeks, together with 'Danaeans' and 'Argives' in the Homeric epic. In recent years, evidence has been found for their existence during the Bronze Age in Anatolia and Northern Syria. Achaea (in Hittite 'Ahhiyawa') in the Bronze Age was a kingdom to the west of the Hittite kingdom, mentioned in Hittite documents from the time of Suppiluliuma I (1380-1346 BCE). It is not known whether it was located on the Greek mainland or in the Aegean Sea. There is an account of the arrival of members of the royal Achaean family to study the art of chariot making during the period of Murshili II (1340-1300 BCE) and bring a statue of

We shall see below how these two issues are intertwined. The information given us by the Bible about the weaponry of Goliath will shed light on his identity, and on the time and circumstances in which the story was composed. They will also help to investigate other foreign personalities mentioned in the Bible and clarify the ideological factors that underlie the editing of some of the stories about the period of the judges and the monarchic period.

---

their god to Hattusha. During the reign of Tudhaliya IV (1250-1220 BCE) there is an account of their invasion of the cities and vassal states of the Hittites. After the decline of the Hittites at the end of the Bronze Age, neo-Hittite kingdoms were established in Anatolia and Northern Syria. In 1997 a Luwian-Phoenician inscription was found of the 9th-8th century BCE in Cilicia that relates about the Kingdom of Hiyawa ('dannym' in Phoenician), and about Adana's king, Warika/Awariku of the Mopsus family. The Greeks credited the hero Mopsus of Colophon in Ionia with the founding of the cities in Pamphylia and Cilicia after the Battle of Troy. According to Xanthus of Lydia he also founded Ashqelon. Warika is also known from the documents of Tiglath-Pileser III and Sargon II. In 2003, in Cincöy near Aleppo, a monumental statue was found of the Storm God. In an inscription on its base, Warika boasts that he extended the borders of 'the Hiyawa plain'. It seems that Hiyawa is connected with ancient Ahhiyawa, and that there was a migration of Achaeans from Western Anatolia to Cilicia (Hawkins 2009: 164-173). In the excavations of Tell Ta'yinat in the Amuq plain, a Luwian inscription was found that decorated the seat of a colossal statue of the ruler, only the head of which survives. The inscription tells about the Wadasatini Kingdom, which was destroyed by Tiglath-Pileser II in 738 BCE. Another inscription from the temple of the Storm God in Halab, wich was discovered in the fortress of Halab in 2003, tells about the hero, Taita, King of Padasatini. Scholars read the name of the kingdom as Palastini – Philistinian. But the precise period of Taita is not yet clear, in the range between the 12th and the 9th centuries BCE. According to Harison it was a powerful Luwian-Aegean Syrian kingdom (Harison 2012).

C. The defensive armament of Goliath and conclusions about his identity and name

C.1. The ethos of military arms and shields in Greece and Israel

David and Goliath represent the opposing ethos of two peoples engaged in war over the Land of Israel. These two ethical systems were formed centuries before the final editing of the story. The key to understanding them are the arms with which each side approached the struggle and the way it was described in the narrative. The Iliad, the Aegean war epic, regarded the high quality of arms as an assurance for a high standard of warfare. The possession of arms raised a man to the level of wealth and power. Sarpedon, the Lycian king says that the Lycian kings are chosen 'seeing they fight amid the foremost Lycians.' (*Iliad* XII: 320-321). The best of the warriors were the leaders of their people equipped with chariots and horses and with excellent armor. The Trojans distribute their arms before the battle according to Hector's instructions: 'And who so is a man, staunch in fight, but hath a small shield on his shoulder, let him give it to a worser man, and himself harness him in a large shield. And going throughout all the host, they made exchange of battle-gear. In good armour did the good warrior harness him, and to the worse they gave the worse' (ibid. XIV: 376-382). The perfect defensive panoply of superb beauty was sent from heaven to the ideal hero Achilles: a shield, armor, helmet and greaves, made by Hephaestus, the blacksmith of Olympus. It is in fact the axis round which the plot turns, and which determined the fate of the Trojans and Achaeans. With it Achilles vanquished Hector in the decisive duel, and by doing so also brought about his own death. Ajax, because of its loss in the contest with Odysseus, committed suicide, and even in the Underworld he did not forgive his rival (*Iliad* XVIII: 478-617; *Odyssey* XI: 543-565).

In the Greek army during the Archaic and Classical periods, more value was given to the hoplites carrying heavy armor, while the fighters without armor were considered as inferior and were called γυμνῆτες (naked). They wore clothes made of cloth or leather, and flung stones from slings or small arrows. Herodotus even used the term 'γυμνῆτες' to describe the choice Persian fighters in the battle of Plataea who fled from the Spartans: the fact that they did not have armor over their clothes was the most dangerous for them - 'πρὸς γὰρ ὁπλίτας ἐόντες γυμνῆτες ἀγῶνα ἐποιεῦντο' (because they fought naked against the hoplites) (Herodotus IX.63.2). Aristagoras of Miletus in the year 500 BCE persuaded the Athenians to help the Ionians who had rebelled against Darius. He promised them that they would easily defeat the Persians since they were not armed with shields and spears (ibid. V.97). According to the Bible, the Philistines relied on the technological advantage of their weaponry, and also zealously guarded their monopoly over metal working.[16] The Israelites used their farming implements as arms, and it is told about Shamgar the son of Anath that he slew six hundred Philistines with an ox goad (Judges 3: 31). And at the

---

[16] Although McNutt's refute this claim, and modern researchers view, based on it, that the Philistines were technologically superior to the Israelites and that they were responsible for introducing to them the knowledge of iron technology. Her study shows that iron tools and weapons were found also in non-Philistine sites from the 12th-10th centuries BCE (1990: 143-205).

beginning of the reign of Saul: 'Now there was no smith found throughout all the land of Israel: for the Philistines said, Lest the Hebrews make them swords or spears. But all the Israelites went down to the Philistines, to sharpen every man his share, and his coulter, and his ax, and his mattock ... So it came to pass in the day of battle, that there was neither sword nor spear found in the hand of any of the people ... but with Saul and with Jonathan his son was there found' (I Samuel 13: 19-22). In the battle of the Elah Valley, Jonathan had only a bow and arrows, a sword, a girdle, and a garment. After the duel he took them off and gave them to David (I Samuel 18: 4). The garment was made of cloth, as in the description of the man of Benjamin after the defeat at Ebenezer: '...with his clothes rent, and with earth upon his head' (I Samuel 4: 12). Only Saul had a helmet and armor, but only the helmet was said to be of bronze. From the verse: '... the shield of Saul, as though he had not been anointed with oil' (II Samuel 1:21). It seems that the shield was made of wood covered with leather and not metal. Unlike David, Jonathan and the rest of the people who were armed for the attack, Saul had confidence in his armor. This did not help him because God had deserted him. He was defeated in the Battle of Gilboa and committed suicide.

In Israel, as among other nations in that region, a war between peoples was conceived like a war between their gods. If they were defeated, this meant that their god was angry with them because they had sinned before him (as it is written, for example, in the stele inscription of Mesha, King of Moab). The inadequate weaponry of the Israelites, which was due to the exigencies of their nomadic days, their settlement, and early monarchy period, is often presented in the Bible as an ideology. David says to Goliath: '... not with sword and spear; for the battle is the Lord's' (I Samuel 17: 47). The victory of the Israelites in battle when they were inferior to their enemies in arms proved that God was on their side and that they were fighting His battle against His enemies. Samson, whose divine power was contained in the locks of his hair, fought the Philistines with empty hands. His predestined calling – '... and he shall begin to deliver Israel out of the hand of the Philistines' (Judges 13:5) – was completed by David who also overcame the lion and bear empty-handed, and to battle Goliath he took primitive weapons from nature: a stick and smooth stones from a brook.

The Bible, which is usually reticent about external appearance, gives many details about the size and weight of Goliath's armor. He was laden with the instruments of assault: a spear, a sword and a dagger. But the sense of his superiority came mainly from his hermetic armor: the shield carried before him, the heavy armor, the helmet and the greaves. Therefore he was confident in his immunity from any injury by man or god. For forty days he would go out and stand at the edge of the Israelite camp, challenge them to a duel and curse their gods. They were filled with terror at his appearance, and when he drew nearer to their ranks they fled for their lives. There was no warrior among them armored like him and taught the arts of war from his youth. Among the Greeks, coping in single combat was highly valued, as we see in the Iliad. In Plato's *Laches*, Nikias, the Athenian commander recommended 'to teach the skill (of fighting in armor in single combats) to our young men... this science will make any man individually a great deal bolder and braver in war... it will give him a smarter appearance (and)...he will appear more terrible to the enemy because of his smartness' (182 b-d).

C.2. The development of hoplite armor

Even those scholars who claim that the description of Goliath's arms is eclectic agree that many items have parallels with the Aegean world. The Homeric epic of the 8th century BCE is the earliest and most detailed literary evidence. In the Iliad the Achaeans, Trojans and their allies wear armor, helmets and greaves made of copper (by the word copper - χαλκός - the intended meaning is 'bronze' as it is in the Bible). Armor in Greek is called θώραξ (the torso), because it mainly protected this upper part of the body. The most widespread terms for warriors was 'brazen coated' and 'the well-greaved'. Ares, the god of war, is called Ἄρης χάλκεος (brazen Ares). But his armor was useless when Diomedes wounded him with the help of Athena: 'Next Diomedes, good at war-cry, drave at Ares with his spear of bronze, and Pallas Athene sped it mightily against his nether-most belly, where he was girded with his taslets. There did he thrust and smite him, rending the fair flesh, and forth he drew the spear again. Then brazen Ares bellowed loud' (*Iliad* V: 855-856). In the Iliad, as in the duel between David and Goliath, there are armored warriors who are wounded or killed by a thrown stone (ibid. V: 99; XIV: 409-413).

The Iliad describes armor of various kinds such as those that protect the chest and the back, or also the loins and the shoulders, while some protected only the chest. They were sometimes made of two metal plates joined together, or from metal strips. The armor of Diomedes was made of flexible metal rings through which a spear penetrated (ibid. V: 113). This wide variety reflects the fact that the warriors were or various peoples from all corners of the Aegean world. Another reason for the variety is that every warrior was armored in his own particular way according to his ability and means. The heaviest investment for protection and decoration was the armor and the shield. The higher the rank of the warrior the more superb and magnificent was his armor. The finest of all was the armor of Achilles which was made by Hephaestus (ibid. XVIII: 481). Researchers of the Iliad are divided in their opinion as to how to translate *thorax* armor. James pointed out the problematic practice of translating it into the names of armor of later periods such as 'corselette' and 'cuirass' (James 2009). Leaf, who thought that the term 'thorax' referred to the armor of the classical hoplite, inferred from this that any mention of this in the Iliad was the addition by later editors (Leaf 1960: 577-578). But the word 'to-ra-ke' is already mentioned in the Linear B tablets of Pylos (Bernabé 2007: 19-20). Homer describes the warfare methods of the Mycenaean world, but some of the details about arms and armor were taken from his own period and mingled with those from earlier ones. The shields as high as towers were typical of the Mycenaean world, while the greaves were widespread only from the 7th century BCE.

From archaeological finds it appears that during the Mycenaean period three types of armor were used. The first was made entirely of bronze plates that protected the warrior in front and back. A protective battle-dress πανοπλία (from παν + ὅπλον) which reached the hips, from the last third of the 15th century BCE, was discovered in a grave in Dendra near Argos. The second type, which was much rarer, was the scale armor. Metal scales, mainly of bronze, were attached on leather or cloth. Bronze scales were also found attached to bronze armor (Snodgrass 1964: 85). In a grave in Phaistos of the 13th century

BCE, bronze scales were found (Galling 1965: 162). The third type was armor made of parallel metal strips (Asimakopoulos 1994: 106).

The manufacture of bronze armor ceased in Greece during the 'Dark Ages' (11th-9th centuries BCE), and instead soldiers wore armor made of cloth or leather; but the Homeric epic shows that their memory was preserved (Snodgrass 2006: 310). They appear once again at the beginning of the Archaic period. It was also then that the phalanx warfare tactic was developed. It appears that the renewed manufacture of bronze armor was the result, on one hand, of migration movements and the contact of Greeks with the metal working of Central Europe and Italy, and on the other hand, of contacts with Assyrians who reached the east shores of the Mediterranean during the reign of Tiglath-Pileser III (745-727 BCE). The armor, greaves and elbow guards, the helmet that in Greece was called 'Corinthian', and the shield with the arm strap and the hand grip were a Greek improvement of the Assyrian, Urartian and Eastern types. The hoplite panoply was therefore an amalgam from different periods and regions, and the Greeks were the ones who drew them together and combined them into the phalanx tactic. The battle-dress was first portrayed in full on proto-Corinthian pottery of 675 BCE, and the phalanx tactic on that of 650 BCE. The hoplites mainly wore armor composed of two concave bronze plates called γύαλα (at the beginning of the Archaic period the word was pronounced as 'guala' but from about 600 BCE it was pronounced 'giala', see below Section C.5). The word is from 'γυη' (curved or hollow) (Kirk 1990: 65), and therefore the armor was called γυαλαθώραξ (gualthorax, and from 600 BCE gialathorax). Its protection value exceeded that of all the other types of armor for hundreds of years. It is already mentioned in Homer (e.g. *Iliad* V: 99; XV: 531; XVII: 314). Pausanias in the 2nd century CE describes a mural of Polygnotus of the 5th century BCE in Delphi depicting the sailing of the Greeks from the ruins of Troy: 'On the altar lies a bronze armor. In our days such armor is rare, but they were commonly used in early times. They are made of two bronze plates, one suited to the chest and stomach and the other protecting the back, which is called γύαλα, and are fastened together by clasps. They considered them as providing sufficient protection and even eliminate the need for a shield. Homer relates that Phorkys the Phrygian did not have a shield because he wore a γυαλαθώραξ[17] ... Caliphon of Samos painted in the Temple of Artemis in Ephesus the portrait of a woman fastening the γύαλα of Patroclus' (10.26:5-6). The length of the γυαλαθώραξ reached down to the waist. In research it is called the 'bell corselette' because its edges turn outwards as the edges of a bell. Later on a convex metal plate or bronze discs were connected the bottom edges to protect the stomach, loins and hips. Sometimes bronze sleeves were added to the shoulders and arms (Ducray 1986: 52-57). Scale armor (φολιδωτός θώραξ) was widespread mainly among the Greeks in the Crimean Peninsula Crete and Cyprus. In Greece itself it was less in evidence than the γυαλαθώραξ but it is also portrayed frequently in art **(fig. 4-10)**.

---

[17] Pausanias quotes from the Iliad XVII: 312-315 the description of the plate armor of Phorkys the Phrygian.

Fig. 4. Bronze 'bell corselette' and high-crest helmet.
Date: late 8th century BCE. Findspot: tomb from late 8th century BCE, Argos, Greece. Argos Museum, No. ANC277226. Drawing: Margalit Levitan.

Fig. 5. Centauromachia.
Pottery: black-figured neck-amphora. Date: 520-500 BCE. Made in Attica. Findspot: Vulci, Lazio, Italy. The British Museum, No. 1836,0224.119. © The Trustees of the British Museum.
The Centauromachy was the battle between the Lapiths and Centaurs at the wedding of the Lapith king Peirithous. A Centaur to left tramples on a Lapith, and raises a white rock in his arms to hurl upon him. The Lapith is fallen backwards to left; he is bearded and fully armed, with high-crested helmet, 'bell corselette', short embroidered chiton, parameridia, and Boeotian shield on right arm, in left hand a white stone.

Fig. 6. Achilles killing the Amazon Queen Penthesilea.
Pottery: black-figured amphora. Date: 530-525 BCE (circa). Made in Attica.
Findspot: Vulci, Lazio, Italy. The British Museum, No. 1836,0224.127. © The Trustees of the British Museum.
Penthesilea brought her Amazon warriors to help the Trojans defend their city, but was killed in combat with Achilles. Achilles's head is protected by his helmet; Penthesilea's helmet is pushed back to expose her features and emphasize her vulnerability. Her spear passes harmlessly across Achilles's chest, while his pierces her throat and blood spurts out. The vase is signed by Exekias as potter. The painting has also been attributed to him.

Fig. 7. Combat of hoplites.
Pottery: black-figured neck-amphora. Date: 540 BCE (circa). Made in Attica. Findspot: Vulci, Lazio, Italy. The British Museum, No. 1843,1103.19. © The Trustees of the British Museum.
On the left is a warrior to right, transfixing with spear another who is beaten down on one knee, and looks back, interposing his shield. Another warrior on the right comes up to his defense, and thrusts at the first with his spear. All are fully armed; the fallen one has a high-crested helmet and shield painted white; the other two have Boeotian shields, that on the right having the device of a tripod.

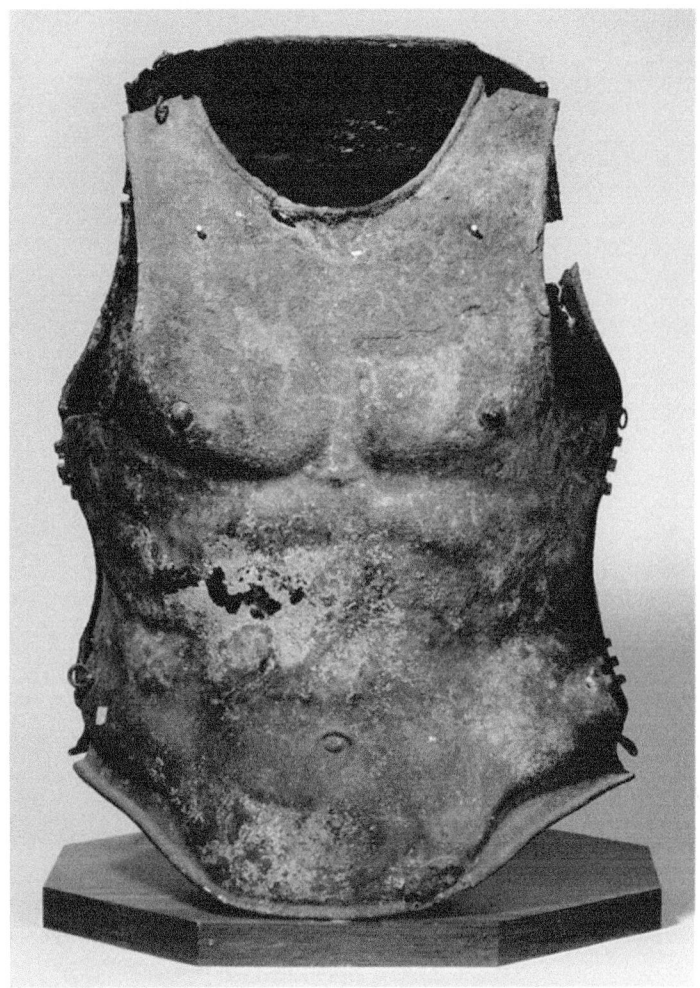

Fig. 8. Bronze plate cuirass.
Date: 4th century BCE. Findspot: Ruvo, Puglia, Italy. The British Museum, No. 1856,1226.61. © The Trustees of the British Museum.

Fig. 9. Menelaos pursuing Helen.
Pottery: red-figured amphora. Date: 470-450 BCE. Made in Attica. Attributed to The Altamura Painter. Findspot: Vulci, Lazio, Italy. The British Museum, No. 1837,0609.71. © The Trustees of the British Museum.
Menelaus pursuing Helen and startled by her beauty. Menelaus, a bearded warrior in helmet, short chiton, and cuirass, and carrying shield (seen in foreshortening) on left arm, drops his sword from his right hand, as, pursuing Helen to right, he recognizes her. She turns as she flies, looking at him and raising her right hand in surprise. The scale armor of Menelaus has a four-rayed star on each shoulder-piece and on the breast one of sixteen rays.

Fig. 10. Bronze Corinthian helmet and pair of greaves.
Date: 520-480 BCE (circa). Findspot: Ruvo, Puglia, Italy. The British Museum, No. 1856,1226.710. © The Trustees of the British Museum.

C.3. Comparison between the armor of Goliath and the hoplite armor

Previous studies have dealt extensively with the panoply of Goliath and its resemblance to Greek panoply of different periods. However, several details still need to be examined:

C.3.1. The armor of Goliath and its heavy weight

According to Galling, who claims that the duel was a 'legend', the size and heavy weight of Goliath's weapons were meant to suit the proportions of a giant in order to stress that he was invincible (1965: 155, 159). But even according to Garsiel, who claims the event was real, the Bible exaggerates in describing Goliath in order to present him as exceptionally terrifying, 'with special physical aspects and carrying an equipment of arms that is unique for its quality and power' (2007: 30). The Bible relates that the weight of Goliath's armor was five thousand shekels of bronze. Malamat estimates this as approximately 36 kg (2007: 18). From the 450 stone weights of the 8th to 6th centuries BCE found in excavations in Judaea, it appears that the weight system was based on the shekel which weighed 11.33 grams (Kletter 2001). According to this, the armor of Goliath weighed about 56 kg.

What was the weight of the hoplite armor? Over time, there was a tendency for the panoply to lighten. The hoplites of the 7th century BCE wore much heavier armor than their 5th and 4th centuries BCE counterparts (Trundle 2004: 122). Vaughn estimates that at the beginning of the 4th century BCE it weighed about 32 kg (1991: 39). But much heavier armor also existed then. Plutarch records that the weight of the armor of Alcimus, a warrior in the army of Demetrius, was about 45 kg (*Demetrius* 21.4). The armor of Agathocles, the tyrant of Syracuse, was so heavy that no one else but he could wear it (Diodorus 19.3.2). Generals such as Xenophon and Philopoemen who tried to march wearing armor were nearly killed by their weight (*Anabasis*, 3.4.48; Plutarch, *Philopoemen*, 6.3-4). Many hoplites who were wounded in battle and fell on each other were crushed or smothered to death under the weight of their armor (Vaughn 1991: 39-41). Fallen armored hoplites are also described in the Iliad (IV: 517-544;XXI: 407), and this is what happened to Goliath when he fell stunned, helpless and unable to move. During the Archaic and Classical periods there are innumerable descriptions of armor with exceptional weight that brought disaster upon their bearers. From this we may deduce both that the Bible did not exaggerate very much in the weight of the armor, and that the situation was not rare or unique. The prophet Jeremiah also describes how the hoplites wearing 'הַסִּרְיֹנֹת' hasiryonot (the armors) of Apries were defeated by Nebuchadnezzar: 'He made many to fall, yea, one fell upon another…' (Jeremiah 46: 16).

C.3.2. The shield bearer of Goliath

According to the Bible, the צִנָּה tsina was heavier than the מָגֵן magen (almost four times as much according to I Kings 10: 16-17, and twice as much according to II Chronicles 9: 16), and it seems that it was very much larger than it. In the Iliad, the hero Ajax had a shield plated with bronze 'taller than a tower' (Iliad VII: 219; XI: 485; XVII: 128). The shield of Hector covered his body from neck to ankles (ibid. VI: 118-119). In the hoplite army, every soldier, even the poorest, had a ὑπασπιστής who bore his shield to the battlefield and handed it over at the last moment before the confrontation (see examples in Hanson 1994: 61-62). In the Battle of Lechaion in 391 BCE, heavily armed and slow moving Spartan hoplites were destroyed in a surprise attack by Athenian peltastai, and left alive only the wounded that the shield bearers had removed at the beginning of the battle (Xenophon, Hellenica, 4.5.11). Sometimes the hoplite and his ὑπασπιστής were separated during the battle, as happened to Xenophon when his men were attacked by a barrage of stones. The hoplite Eurylochus came to his aid and protected both of them from the stones with his shield and they retreated thus together (Anabasis, 4.2.20-21). The shield bearer of Goliath is not mentioned at the moment of confrontation. But this was not because he kept away from the field of battle before the duel, as Garsiel inferred from the fact that he did not come to the aid of his master (2009: 62), but simply because he did not manage to pass the shield to him in time because of David's diversionary tactics and surprise attack. It even says explicitly that he approached David together with Goliath – in fact one step ahead of him: 'And the Philistine came on and drew near unto David; and the man that bare the shield went before him' (I Samuel 17: 41).

The Bible says that the height of the Philistine was six cubits and a span (2.92m). It may be that the biblical estimate included the full height of that 'war machine'. The length of the hoplite spear that included a wooden handle and an iron blade (which from the 7th century BCE replaced the bronze blade) was as much as 2.7m and even more (Hanson 1991: 22-24). The height of the warriors had a psychological effect. In the Iliad its says that they aroused fear in their opponents with the waving of their long spears and the high crest of their helmets.[18]

C.3.3. The helmet of Goliath

The helmet made of bronze well protected the head of the warrior. When Diomedes thrust his spear at the head of Hector, 'on the top of the helmet, but the bronze was turned aside by bronze, and reached not his fair flesh' (*Iliad* XI: 350-354). Galling thinks that Goliath had an Assyrian helmet without protection for the forehead and nose, which allowed the sling stone to penetrate his forehead. Garsiel also things that the helmet left the eyes, mouth, nose and part of his face and forehead exposed (2007: 33). In the Septuagint, the translators apparently thought that this was a hoplite helmet with forehead protection, since they added the words 'δια της περικεφαλαίας' (through the helmet) to the description of the penetration of the sling stone. But even if we do not accept this addition, it is still possible that the biblical author described this kind of helmet. The type of 'Corinthian helmet', which was very widespread, gave maximum protection in covering the forehead,

---

[18] The importance of the height of the warrior is reflected in the fact that Saul was head and shoulders taller than anyone among the people. But his advantage, just like all physical and technological advantages in the Bible, was of little value when God abandoned him. He wore armor and a helmet like the Philistines, but he did not dare to fight them. His anointing as king was proved to have been a mistake. The vanity of material things and external appearance is also stressed in the anointing of David, the little shepherd boy, as king. He was chosen even though he was youngest of his brothers, and his father and brothers belittled his value. God tells Samuel, who tended towards Eliav the eldest son: 'Look not on his countenance, or on the height of his stature: because I have refused him: for the Lord seeth not as man seeth; for man looketh on the outward appearance, but the Lord looketh on the heart' (I Samuel 16: 7). There is also a parallel with Jacob (Israel) the shepherd and Esau the mighty hero, whose father Isaac also mistook their value.

nose and ears. But this was heavy, hot and greatly limited the field of vision and sound. Therefore, in the 7th century BCE, an improvement was made to it that allowed it to be raised back on the head until the beginning of the battle (Snodgrass 2006: 356; Hanson 1991: 74-75). Numerous works of art describe warriors in this way not only at the moment of battle but also during its course **(Figs. 11-13).** Thus a warrior fighting next to Athena is portrayed in the west pediment reliefs of the temple of Athena Aphaia in Aegina (around 490 BCE). The sculptor Kresilas (around 430 BCE) thus portrayed Athena the goddess of war (known as the 'Velletri type'), as well as Pericles as a *strategos* in the famous herm that he made. It seems that the helmet of Goliath was pushed back because he wanted to see his opponent and speak to him. He did not think he would already be attacked at the psychological warfare stage of exchanging taunts and curses.

C.4 Diversionary tactics

The staff that David carried was a decoy weapon to divert the attention of his opponent from the real weapon, the sling stone that was concealed in his shoulder bag (I Samuel, 17: 40). Goliath focused on the staff and assumed that David intended to hold close combat with him: 'And the Philistine said to David, Am I a dog that you come to me with staves?' (17: 43). This is known as 'change blindness': the diversion of attention by a visual stimulus which causes one to overlook another visual stimulus that is also at the center of the visual field (Mack 1992: 475-501).

Diversionary tactics such as those of David were commonly practiced among hoplite battles. In Greek it was called στρατήγημμα (stratagems). Diogenes Laertius (1.74), Strabo (13.1.37) and Polyaenus (1.26) tell about the war that was conducted at the end of the 7th century BCE between Athens and Mytilene in Lesbos for control over Sigeion, which they decided to resolve by a duel. The Athenian commander Phrynon fought against a fisherman called Pittacus, who later became the tyrant of Mytilene (650-570 BCE). Phrynon was an Olympic champion in *pankration* (a martial art that included boxing and wrestling). But Pittacus ran towards Phrynon, trapped him with his fishing net and killed him with a trident and a dagger.

There is a clear resemblance between this story and the story of David and Goliath in the decisive duel motif between a professional and fearsome hoplite and a γυμνήτης who used his working tools in a running and surprise attack. In general, there are also similarities between the plots of the two events. Pittacus also wins the acclaim of the people for his victory, and was elected to rule over Lesbos in spite of his low and foreign origins (his mother was Thracian and David's great-grandmother was Ruth the Moabite). To him belongs the apophthegm, 'καιρό γίγνωσκε' (know thy opportunity) (Diogenes Laertius I.79). This was indeed a duel that raised the poor fisherman and the little shepherd to rule. Pittacus married, as did David, into the family of the previous ruler Penthilus. David rebuked Michal for her arrogance. Pittacus also accused his wife of arrogance, and his simple ways earned him scorn by the aristocrats such as the poet Alcaeus who boasted of the victory of his brother in a duel with a giant, perhaps to compete with the glory of Pittacus (see below, Section F.2). Pittacus, like David, was a poet, and was listed among the Seven Sages of Greece.[19] The exploits of Pittacus and Alcaeus occurred and were told

---

[19] His famous saying is: 'Do not do to your neighbor what is hateful to you' (*Pittacus* fragment 10.3). This

FIG. 11. HOPLITE.
MARBLE RELIEF (BLOCK XXVII) FROM THE NORTH FRIEZE OF THE PARTHENON. DESIGNED BY: PHEIDIAS. DATE: 438-432 BCE. FINDSPOT: ACROPOLIS, ATHENS, GREECE. THE BRITISH MUSEUM, NO. 1816,0610.29-30.A. © THE TRUSTEES OF THE BRITISH MUSEUM.
THE FRIEZE SHOWS THE PROCESSION OF THE PANATHENAIC FESTIVAL, THE COMMEMORATION OF THE BIRTHDAY OF THE GODDESS ATHENA. THE HELMET OF THE FOOT SOLDIER WITH ITS HORSE HAIR CREST, THE BODY ARMOR AND THE UPPER PART OF HIS SHIELD ARE WELL PRESERVED.

FIG. 12. ARCHER AND COMBAT OF HOPLITES.
MARBLE RELIEF. PART OF THE FIRST FRIEZE, WHICH IS THE LOWER, LARGER FRIEZE AT TOP OF THE PODIUM OF THE NEREID MONUMENT LOWER FRIEZE OF THE NEREID MONUMENT. DATE: 400 BCE (CIRCA). FINDSPOT: XANTHUS, ASIA MINOR (TURKEY). THE BRITISH MUSEUM, NO. 1848,1020.35. © THE TRUSTEES OF THE BRITISH MUSEUM.
ON THE LEFT OF THIS SLAB AN ARCHER IS DRAWING A BOW TOWARDS THE RIGHT. HE WEARS A TUNIC BELTED AT THE WAIST AND A CHLAMYS AND HAS A QUIVER BESIDE HIS LEFT THIGH. TO THE RIGHT TWO HOPLITES CLASH SHIELD AGAINST SHIELD. THEY RAISE THEIR RIGHT HANDS TO THRUST WITH THEIR SPEARS. THE HOPLITE ON THE LEFT WEARS A HELMET, CUIRASS, TUNIC AND CHLAMYS. THE ONE ON THE RIGHT CAN BE SEEN TO WEAR A HELMET, TUNIC AND CHLAMYS.

FIG. 13. BUST OF PERICLES.
MARBLE PORTRAIT BUST OF PERICLES. DATE: 2ND CENTURY AD. FINDSPOT: TIVOLI, LAZIO, ITALY. THE BRITISH MUSEUM, NO. 1805,0703.91. © THE TRUSTEES OF THE BRITISH MUSEUM MARBLE PORTRAIT BUST. PERICLES WEARING A HELMET PUSHED BACK ON HIS HEAD. A ROMAN COPY OF AN EARLIER GREEK ORIGINAL. THE NAME IS INSCRIBED IN GREEK.

at the turn of the 7th century BCE, just when the story of the duel between David and Goliath was compiled.

Hoffmeier recently claimed that by cutting off Goliath's head, David was acting according to accepted practice in the Middle East and not in the Greek world. In his opinion David brought the head of Goliath to Jerusalem when it was still in the hands of the Jebusites to show them that this would be their fate. He brings examples of the brutal and macabre treatment of the dead bodies of enemies in Egypt and Assyria, such as beheading them and displaying them publicly, as well as dragging them behind the chariot of the victor. In his opinion, the Greeks did not behave in this way, and as evidence he quotes Hector who wishes for the proper treatment of his body (*Iliad* VII: 85-89) (2011: 103-109). However, let us recall, that Achilles dragged the body of Hector tied to his chariot for twelve days around the monument to Patroclus. Priam asks whether Achilles severed the limbs of Hector and threw them to the dogs, as he had threatened to do (*Iliad* XXII: 335-336; XXIV: 409). Beheadings during duels are mentioned in the Iliad. Agammenon beheaded Hippolochus, and Diomedes beheaded Dolon (ibid. V: 454-457; IX: 146-147). The Israelites also severed the limbs of the defeated, and their bodies were discarded as food for dogs (Judges 1: 6; II Kings 9: 10). But this is not how David behaved. He did not cut off the head of Goliath to abuse it, but only in the course of the duel when there remained the danger he would recover from his shock and rise up again. The massive armor was perhaps difficult for the sword to penetrate, but it did not cover the throat and the nape. In the Iliad as well, Athena threw a stone and struck the neck of Ares who collapsed and fell (*Iliad* XXI: 403-406).

To sum up, it seems that the biblical author saw before him the figure of the Aegean hoplite of his time and the way he fought. The πρόμαχος who fought in the arena of the το μεταίχμιον, the shield bearer, the greaves that were common from the 7th century BCE, the weight of the armor that resembled the heavy hoplite armor, and the helmet that Goliath pushed back until the moment he planned to begin the close combat. In my opinion, the armor of Goliath allows us to determine the meaning of his name. The personal name of the Philistine warrior was forgotten in the course of time, and in the final recension of the story was named after the item most typical of the hoplite, the massive superbly fashioned armor which for centuries had become known for its excellent strength and endurance.

Finkelstein noticed that the story of David and Goliath was shaped by the Deut. historian in the spirit of his time. We should note that also in the visual arts events and personalities of earlier times are often described in contemporary dress and according to current interpretation. In the series of David stories pictured in the Dura Europos synagogue of the 3rd century CE the characters are dressed in Graeco-Roman himation. Yavetz maintained that the *Zeitgeist* (the spirit of the times) influenced all historical writing:

---

is a central principle in Judaism: 'Thou shalt love thy neighbor as thyself' (Leviticus 19:18). See: *Jerusalem Talmud*, 'Nedarim' 30b. Hillel the Elder says: 'What is hateful to you – do not do to your friend. This is the whole Torah…' (*Babylonian Talmud*, 'Shabbat', 31a). The same appears in Christianity (Matthew 19; Mark 12; Paul, 'To the Romans', 13). Kurke interprets the words of Diogenes Laertius, that Pittacus consecrated the land given him by the Mythilenaes, and which until his day was called Πιττάκειος (belonging to Pittacus) (D.L. 1, 75), as testimony of the cult of Pittacus in his *temenos* (sanctuary) in the center of Mytilene as their founding hero and restorer (1994: 192). This resembles the historical-religious status of David.

'Every historian of the past is a citizen of the present. We learn from the past about the present, just as we learn from the present about the past' (2002, Vol. I: 11-26). As Carr says, in order to understand the present, we have to go back to the past. Our very view of the problem *What is history?* is dictated to us by our position along the continuum of time (1962: 5, 69). We also tend to shape his story in line with our interests and aspirations. Arieli presents the debate that has existed since the days of Ancient Greece until our own times between historiographical schools. Is every event and historical situation unique and irreversible and can not be generalized, and therefore the study of the past is done for 'its own sake', or is history and its study a practical and necessary tool to understand the present, to cope with it and to change it (1992: 1-33). In biblical historiography there is no detachment between the past and the present. Kaduri discussed the motives of the biblical commentators who began their activity after the destruction of the First Temple and especially during the years of the Return to Zion, which were to find in the holy scriptures the guidance for the life of people in the present and to shape its future (2011: 3-9). Yefet wrote about the author of the Book of Chronicles during the Second Temple period: 'It seems that most of the accusations against him – that he describes the past from the viewpoint of his contemporary interests; that he is worried about the problems of identity and legitimacy peculiar to his period; that what interests him really is the future of the people of Israel; that he writes within the context of philosophical outlooks and moral values; and so on – all these are in fact the authentic characteristics of all historical writing in itself' (2004: 14). Thompson noted that the late editing of the collection of traditions in the Bible was motivated more by the needs of contemporary society than an interest in the past *per se*. (1992: 381-382). Funkenstein pointed out the typological-symbolical thinking in the Bible which finds symbolic-structural analogies between events, people and institutions of different periods. It comprises a sense of identification with an actual segment of the past, a sense of rejection of the past and of the eschatological completion of the past. This is how the exodus from Egypt was perceived as a paradigm for redemption (for example in Isaiah 11:15-16). The golden calf of Jeroboam was identified with the golden calf at Mount Sinai (I Kings: 12-28). The identification of those returning to Zion in the days of Ezra and Nehemiah with the generation of the conquest of Canaan is given liturgical expression: 'And all the congregation of them that were come again out of the captivity made booths, and sat under the booths; for since the days of Jeshua the son of Nun unto that day had not the children of Israel done so. And there was very great gladness' (Nehemiah 8: 17) (1991: 157-159).

C.5. How did 'γυαλαθώραξ' turn into 'Goliath'

In the Greek world, the phonology of γύαλα/γυαλαθώραξ was different in every place and time because of the phonological development of the upsilon Y/υ. This first corresponded to the Phoenician ו (wau), which in the ancient Archaic period was written as a V and pronounced as 'ו'(oo/u). From about 600 BCE the Y was written and pronounced as the German *ü* or the French *u*, but was usually pronounced as 'י' as in the English 'i' (only the Boeotians continued to use the earlier phonology). The Aeolians (in Aeolis and Lesbos) used the upsilon instead of the omicron 'O' (e.g. ονύμα instead of ονόμα) and also instead of alpha 'A/a' (κατύ instead of κατά) (Stamatakos 1972: 1020-1021).

Pronunciation of the upsilon as 'י' began therefore from the period in which thousands of Greek mercenaries participated in military campaigns in our region, in which the allies of Judah fought against Babylon; a short while before Judah was destroyed and the 'remnants of Judah' under the leadership of army officers settled in Egypt, in the settlements were the mercenaries dwelled. Therefore the name was entered into the Bible in its revised pronunciation, 'גִיאָלַת-ורקס' (gialath-orax). An additional change occurred when the 'י' 'yod' moved behind the 'למ'ד' 'lamed' and was pronounced 'גָּלְיָת' (galiath), perhaps to make it easier to say. (A change of this kind in the position of the vowel Ἰῶτα - 'I/ι' (which parallels the Phoenician 'yod') is found in the transcription of Ἀχαιος /אָכִיש/אַכַיוֹס into 'Ikausu in Assyrian).

It seems that the Tiberian Vocalisation preserved the biblical pronunciation. The first syllable is קָמַץ קָטָן, ('small qamatz'), a closed syllable which ends in a consonant with שְׁוָא נָח ('shwa nakh'), (zero vowel). It is identical in appearance to the standard qamatz, but is pronounced as a 'o', rather than 'a'. Some other examples besides גָּלְיָת are: תָּכְנִית (program); חָכְמָה (wisdom); כָּל- (all). The editors of the story created a rhyme: שְׁמוֹ מִגַּת גָּלְיָת (Goliath of Gath) by shortening γυαλαθ-ώραξ (or adding ו'תי – 'tav'/th – to the word γύαλα). All these changes caused the origin of the name to be forgotten in the period of the Septuagint translation. Therefore it was not translated back into the Greek term but was written as Γολιαθ. For the same reason the term 'סרנים' was not translated into the original term τύραννοι, but into the contemporary term 'σάτραπας των αλλοφυλων' (since the title and function of the satrap during the period of the Persian Empire, was preserved in the *Diadochi*'s kingdoms).

But if Goliath was fashioned into the figure of a Saitic hoplite, why did the text say he wore scale armor? Finkelstein offers two possible explanations. Some of the mercenaries, especially those of Cyprus origin, wore scale armor, or the Deut. editor mixed into his description some neo-Assyrian motifs. In the opinion of Fantalkin, the Greek mercenaries in the East adopted the local scale armor (2008: 330). He mentions the two armor scales found in Mesad Hashavyahu where the Aegean mercenaries were stationed, and also the wealth of iron scales that were found in the excavations of the Hophra (Apries) palace in Memphis, which served the Pharaohs continuously until they transferred their place of residence to Alexandria during the Ptolemaic period. But Flinders Petrie, the excavator of Memphis, stressed that the scales were from the period of the Persian conquest of Egypt. Iron scale armor has always been commonly found among the Persians. According to Herodotus, the Persians wore armor with sleeves on which there were fish-like scales (VII.6) while the Saitic hoplites wore armor made of large plates. Ammianus Marcellinus of the 4th century CE relates that the Persians were wrapped from head to foot with thin flexible iron plates like the feathers of a bird (XXIV, iv. 15. XXIV.vii, 8). In Egypt it was the custom to wear scale armor from the 18th till the 20th dynasty (between 1580-1085 BCE) (Snodgrass 1964: 85), and figurines of Amenhotep II, Rameses III and Sheshonk I were found wearing it. But the Saitic Pharaoahs are not represented with it (1909: 11, 38). http://www.digitalegypt.ucl.ac.uk/memphis/armours.html_(University College London, 2002). Perhaps because it was customary among the Assyrians from whose conquest they had liberated themselves. While they showed considerable openness towards the Greek world, they turned their backs on Mesopotamia and rejected attempts at closer contact by the Persians (see Section F.1). The Septuagint version, that the scales of Goliath's armor were of bronze and iron, suits the Persian armor with which the translator of the later period was familiar. To sum up, the biblical editor mingled his description with two kinds of armor that were widely known. But the *name* of Goliath was derived from the most massive and well-known armor which typified the Greek hoplite.

D. The name is the message: four proofs

D.1. Parallel instances of a military equipment item turning into a personal name or epithet

Additional Aegean names were adopted in the Bible for military terms. In all languages and periods the name of a professional person has derived from an object that typifies him, and this is also the case with military terms. In Latin, for example, the word gladiator is derived from *gladius* (sword), and in Hebrew the word קַשָּׁת qashat (archer) derives from קֶשֶׁת qeshet (the bow), or רוֹבַאי rovaiy (rifleman) from רוֹבֶה rove (rifle). We use the word טַנְקִיסְט tankist (tank crewman) from טַנְק tank which was not Hebraized. In modern research it is accepted that the name הַפְּלֵתִי plethy (Pelethites), the Aegean body guards of David, is derived from the Greek πελτασταί/πελθασταί, infantrymen carrying a light shield, πέλτη/πέλθε. The term *peltha* originates in Crete (Margalith 1994: 55). Cretan mercenaries appeared in our region from the 6th century BCE. The Bible adopted the name הַפְּלֵתִי but the meaning of the term was forgotten and it was combined with הַכְּרֵתִי until it was considered an ethnonym like Cretans and Carians. We have therefore another late literary invention of an arms item that became a personal name through a play on words and rhyme. This process parallels the turning of the name of an armor into the name of a person, Goliath of Gath. Here, too, the first syllable 'E/ε' epsilon wandered off in the Hebrew transcription and appeared after the second consonant. The phenomenon of calling a person by an item of his military equipment until his original name is forgotten also exists in other periods. Famous examples are the Roman emperor Caligula (his real name was Gaius Julius Caesar) who was named for the *caliga*, the footwear used by soldiers, and Caracalla (his name was Septimius Bassianus Lucius, and his name as emperor was Aurelius Marcus Severus Antoninus Augustus) who was named for the cloak that he introduced into military use.

Personal names or nicknames deriving from military weaponry can be found among the Greeks in ancient times: 'Xiphos' Ξίφος (sword), 'Aspis' (shield), and the most widespread one since the 6th century BCE – 'Thorax' and its derivatives: 'Thorakis' and 'Thorakides' (Fraser & Matthews 1987). One of the mercenaries of Psammaticus II in the Abu-Simbel inscription was called 'Pelekos' Πέλεκος (ax). Masson and Olivier ascribe this to the type of personal names that were derived from weapons of war such as Thorax, and 'Skeparnos' Σκέπαρνος (ax) (Masson & Olivier 1957: 9-10).

The כּוֹבַע/קוֹבַע that appears in the story of the duel is also Aegean in origin. It is generally accepted that the name originates in Hittite: כּוּפָּחִי – kupahi (in Greek κύμβαχος) which means the helmet of a warrior (Tischker 1983: 640-641). The word כִּימְבַּ-כוֹס as in the word גְּיָלָת-וֹרֶקְס the last part was deleted and the words were left with two syllables: כּוֹ-בַע, גָּלְ-יָת. In both of them the upsilon was converted into the vowel pronounced as 'i'/'o'.

Why was the word kupahi/κύμβαχος and not γυαλαθώραξ converted into a Hebrew word in ancient times? The bronze helmet was much cheaper and lighter than the bronze armor, and the Israelites could make use of it and Hebraize its name. In fact, only the helmet of Saul was said to have been made of copper, and not his armor. One may therefore infer the Anatolian origins of the Philistines. But it may also have entered the biblical text from the Greek during the period in which Aegean mercenaries were stationed in the country in service of the Egyptian rulers, as well as the mercenaries of the Kingdom of Judah. Or it may have occurred after the destruction of the Temple when the remnants of Judah migrated to Egypt and lived together with the mercenaries in their cities.

The parallels confirm that it was from the Aegean name of the plate armor, or the hard armor to which metal scales were attached, that the Bible derived the name of the warrior who wore it. This is because it was the most important life-saving item in his armament. It was the most expensive component in his equipment: Expert craftsmen created 140 thousand shields and 140 thousand helmets for the mercenaries of Dionysus, the tyrant of Syracuse, but only 14 thousand pieces of armor which he distributed to the cavalry and to the captains and to the mercenaries in his bodyguard (Diodorus 16.42.2-3). Philip II king of Macedonia confiscated the military equipment of the mercenaries of the Phocians whom he had defeated in 346 B.C. It was, a severe punishment since he stole their future livelihood. Probably he left them only their assault weapons (Diodorus 16.62.2; Trundle 2004: 126). The plate armor was the most important possession to save the life of the hoplite. It protected him even after his spear was broken and also his shield which was made of wood. The plate armor was sometimes so fortified against repeated blows that according to Pausanias it obviated the need to carry a shield (10.26.5). During the period of phalanx warfare, the body of the hoplite which was completely wrapped in bronze became a weapon in himself as he was pushed by the ranks behind him into the ranks of the enemy (Hanson 1994: 88). The armor was the source for the superiority of Goliath over his defenseless enemies, and therefore he was given the name 'armor' or 'the armored one'.

Finkelstein correctly defined the sources of inspiration for the figure of Goliath as the Greek hoplites who served as Saitic mercenaries and the Homeric epic. The realization of Yadin that the Bible used the arms and style of the epic for conducting war against the Greeks and smiting them with their own weapons – also explains the term 'man of armor', since the standard term for the warrior in the Iliad was 'brazen coated'. The bronze armor was well known to all the Greeks from reality and from fictional narratives, and symbolized their strength and technical superiority over the peoples of Asia. The intention of the Bible in giving this epithet was sarcastic: that the humiliation and total defeat of this symbol would be comprehensible to the Greek ear. But how and when was the biblical author aware of the Greek term? Already in the period of the judges the Israelites had come into daily contact with Philistine metalworkers for manufacturing and repairing their agricultural tools. The symbiosis with the Philistines is evident from the exploits of Samson, and David and his men had also served in the army of Achish. The contacts continued even during the days of the Kingdom of Judah, with the significant presence in the 7th century BCE of Greek material culture in the cities of Philistia. The military term may also have come through the mercenaries from Cyprus and Asia Minor who sometimes served the kings of Judah. The term 'gialathorax' which appears for the first time in Homer was perhaps in use even before his time. But the full hoplite battle-dress which included greaves was widespread only from his time onwards. In the 7th and 6th centuries BCE Aegean mercenaries in Israel were a common phenomenon, especially in the war campaigns and conquests of the Saites, and it seems they occupied the forts in the country until its conquest by Babylon (see Section E). In addition, there were contacts between Jews and Greeks in the context of their service as mercenaries in Egypt.[20] There is no doubt that these contacts intensified after the migration of the 'remnants of Judah' (those who were not exiled to Babylon) to Egypt. In the Book of Jeremiah (44: 1; 46: 14) it is written that they settled in the cities where the mercenaries dwelt: Tahpanhes, Noph and Migdol, and must have become familiar with their lifestyle (see Section G).

D.2. The Philistine warrior was nameless

Throughout Chapter 17 the bitter enemy of David and the Israelites is mentioned twenty-three times (!) only with the epithet 'the Philistine', and only once does it say 'Goliath of Gath was his name' (in verse 4). Scholars have not found a sufficient explanation for this. Rofé identified this with the motif of the 'nameless hero' who appeared for a short while in biblical narrative of the Second Temple days (1986: 68-69). But this motif only referred to the anonymous Israelite prophets. Besides which, when this man was allowed to speak he identified himself as: 'Am I not the Philistine?'. Here, and in all the other places, the lacuna of his name is very noticeable. It should have read: 'Am I not *so-and-so* the Philistine?'. How different this is from the explicit calling of the name 'Samuel! Samuel!' And the response: 'Here I am!' which is repeated three times in the same book of I Samuel (Chapter 3). It is clear from this that 'Goliath' was not the real name of the Philistine warrior. In the Homeric epic as well, the heroes before battle usually identify themselves and glorify their ancestry. Why was the name forgotten in this case? It is logical if the story was written a long time after the event. In this same way the name 'Achish', of the ancient king of Gath which had already been destroyed two hundred years earlier, was attached to the king of Ekron in the days of Josiah.

---

[20] The Saite Pharaohs were in need of thousands of foreign mercenaries to liberate their country and guard its borders; to conquer Philistia, the Land of Israel, and Phoenicia; to fight against the Babylonians, and even to impose their authority on their own Egyptian subjects. Herodotus says about their shortage of Egyptian soldiers that during the reign of Psammeticus I, because of the extremely long period of service, 240,000 Egyptian soldiers deserted and went to Nubia (Herodotus II.30). The mercenaries were mostly Greek, but according to the '*Letter of Aristeas*' (2nd century BCE), soldiers were also sent from Judah to assist Psammeticus in his war with the Ethiopians (he meant Nubians) (*Letter of Aristeas*, 12). There is a debate among scholars whether this was Psammeticus I (which means that, according to the time of his wars with the Nubians, the Judaeans were sent by Manasseh at the beginning of this Pharaoh's reign, or at the end of it by Josiah), or Psammeticus II who also fought against the Nubians (Kahn 2007: 507-515; idem 2008: 139-157). Herodotus relates that a number of mercenaries were stationed in the Delta region in στρατόπεδα (army camps) until Amasis transferred them to Memphis, his city (see Section F.1). Petrie and others identify these camps with the fortifications in Tell Daphnae (ancient Daphne Δάφνη), Naucratis (Ναύκρατις), Tell Ballamun (ancient Ἑρμοῦπόλις μικρά), and in the fort of Migdol in northern Sinai, where Greek, Phoenician, and Judaean mercenaries were stationed (Oren 1992: 1111-1112; Williams & Villing 2006: 49). In Upper Egypt (the biblical 'Land of Pathros'), in the island of Yeb (in Greek, Elephantine ελεφάντινη) on the Nubian border, there was a colony of Jewish mercenaries and their families during the 6th and 5th centuries BCE. From a document found in that place it appears that its foundation was prior to the Persian conquest. Perhaps it was originally the place of the auxiliary forces from Judah. Jews also arrived in Egypt with the exile of Jehoahaz by Necho; it may have been even before the arrival of those opposed to the reforms of Josiah, or that they arrived during the thirty years before the destruction of the First Temple (Porten 1968; Yavetz 2002: Vol. 3, 32-35; Rosen 2008: 51-52). Greek mercenaries also arrived in Yeb during the campaign of Psamettichus II against the Nubians, as can be inferred from the inscriptions discovered in Abu Simbel.

D.3. There are multiple 'Goliaths'

This third piece of evidence is brought in from the very place that had always posed a major difficulty for biblical commentators and translators, and that caused many scholars to treat the duel between David and Goliath as a fiction – the parallel story of Elhanan the Bethlehemite who defeated Goliath the son of the giant at Gob. Already in I Chronicles they tried to resolve the difficulty by saying that Elhanan overcame the warrior brother of Goliath of Gath. Rashi says 'Elhanan is David'. Radak explains the meaning of the word 'אֶת' in the verse: 'And ... Elhanan the son of Jaare-oregim, a Bethlehemite, slew Goliath the Gittite' as 'someone who was **with** Goliath the Gittite'. It is reasonable to suppose that this was his brother. From this it seems that Elhanan killed Lahmi the brother of Goliath while David killed Goliath.[21]

Honeyman and many others likewise thought that the text had read 'Elhanan son of Jesse', and the editor in the Persian period when the text was transferred to a square script, mistakenly copied the name 'יִשַׁי' as 'יַעְרֵי' in square script by splitting the letter שׁיִן 'shin' into two letters - עיִ and רִשׁ (1948: 23-25). But if this is so, why did not similar errors occur in copying the Bible, since there are no other places in which the letter שׁיִן was mistakenly separated into עיִ and רִשׁ? Some scholars thought that 'Elhanan' was the real name of David, while the name 'David' originates from the word 'Dawidam' in the Mari documents of the 18th century BCE, which means commander. But Tadmor proves that the 'Dawidam' derives from the Babylonian word 'dabdum' which comes only in the combination 'daku dawidam' and means 'to kill the commander of the defeated enemy' (1958: 129-131). The name דָּוִד David apparently comes from the word דּוֹד dod (uncle) or יָדִיד yadid (friend), the beloved one (Kitchen 1966: 85-86). This means that Elhanan was not David but another hero who defeated another warrior armed with a gialathorax, and not the one that David defeated. This is close to the commentary of Radak, and in view of my explanations above, this is the simplest solution that is acceptable. Confirmation for this is that the Bible says Goliath who was killed by Elhanan also had a special spear

---

[21] The story in II Samuel 21: 18-22 relates that before David ceased participating in wars himself, '...there was again a battle with the Philistines at Gob: then Sibbechai the Hushathite slew Saph, which was of the sons of the giant. And there was again a battle in Gob with the Philistines, where Elhanan the son of Jaare-orgim, a Bethlehemite, slew *the brother of* Goliath the Gittite, the staff of whose spear was like a weavers' (orgim אֹרְגִים) beam. And there was yet a battle in Gath, where was a man of great stature that had on every hand six fingers, and on every foot six toes, four and twenty in number; and he also was born to the giant. And when he defied Israel, Jonathan the son of Shimeah the brother of David slew him. These four were born to the giant in Gath, and fell by the hand of David, and by the hand of his servants'. In I Chronicles 20: 4-8 it says: 'And it came to pass after this, that there arose war at Gezer with the Philistines; at which time Sibbechai the Hushathite slew Sippai, that was of the children of the giant: and they were subdued. And there was war again with the Philistines; and Elhanan the son of Jair slew Lähmi the brother of Goliath the Gittite, whose spear staff was like weavers' beam. And yet again there was war at Gath, where was a man of great stature, who fingers and toes were four and twenty, six on each hand and six on each foot; and he also was the son of the giant. And when he defied Israel, Jonathan the son of Shimea David's brother slew him. These were born unto the giant in Gath; and they fell by the hand of David, and by the hand of his servants'. The explanation in *Targum Jonathan* (Jonathan's Translation) (7th century CE) for the verse in Samuel as 'And David the son of Jesse... whose mother אַרְגֵת weaves the Ark curtain for the Temple with the weavers' beam, killed Goliath whose spear was like a weavers' beam. And he [David, S. R.] was called Elhanan because God showed him grace'. Rashi interprets the verse 'and Elhanan ben Jair slew' as being 'one of David's warriors'. Radak, in his commentary on II Samuel 17 and 21 and I Chronicles 20 says that Goliath the Gittite was Goliath the Philistine who was killed by David, and Elhanan killed Lahmi, the bother of Goliath, with the assistance of David.

with a staff resembling a weaver's beam. In this way the riddle of multiple 'Goliaths' and 'Goliath killers' has been solved because there is no contradiction between them.

Further confirmation are the other Philistine warriors who were engaged in duel by David's warriors, such as Saph/Sipai by Sibbechai the Hushathite; a man of great stature by Jonathan the son of Shimeah; Lähmi the brother of Goliath by Elhanan ben Jair/Jaare; and Ishbi, whose spear weighed three hundred shekels of copper by Abishai the son of Tseruiah. It appears that the Philistine society had a rank of professional warriors, heavily armed and with weapons like those they had used in military training since childhood (like the Spartan warriors). All of them were 'the children of harapha', and they were also of the city of Gath. In the Bible the word 'רְפָאִים' rephaim is mentioned (some derived the term from the Greek word ἅρπη harpe, sword). Like the adjective 'בֶּן-עֲנָת' ben Anath (son of Anath, Goddess of war) that indicates he belongs to the warrior class (from inscriptions on arrowheads from Al-Khader near Bethlehem, in the name of the judge Shamgar ben Anath, and in a seal of the 8th or 7th century BCE of רפא בנענת rpha bn'ant (Heltzer 1994). After being crowned king, David employed, besides the Cherethites and Pelethites, six hundred Philistine warriors from the city of Gath as a select unit commanded by Ittai the Gittite. All of them remained personally loyal to him even when Absalom rebelled against him (II Samuel 15: 18-23). It is possible that 'אִיתַי' Ittai was also not the real name of the Philistine but his epithet as a professional warrior, a mercenary, meaning אִישִׁי (my man, my hired warrior). The letters שׁ/ש 'shin' and ת/ו 'tav' are a pair of letters that interchangeable as in the words תְּלַת-שָׁלַשׁ, תְּרֵי-שְׁנֵי, תּוֹר-שׁוֹר. The memory of the power of Gath which was one of the largest cities in the country before it was destroyed by Hazael, King of Aram, is still preserved in the days of the Deut. author, and from this comes its description as the place where warrior heroes were bred. It is related that Achish himself employed mercenaries. He even employed David and his men, and behaved as though he had not known about David's killing of the best warrior of his city (he once banished him only after his servants 'reminded' him of this, and other time he expelled him from the ranks of his warriors only after Philistine captains castigated him). This may have been because he had used him to get rid of dangerous internal rivals. Talented and popular warriors were considered as potential rivals who threatened their masters, as in the case of David and Saul. In the 7th century BCE, Gyges, a talented warrior in the service of Sadyates, King of Lydia, deposed him and seized the throne. He was the one who began providing mercenaries to the Saite Pharaoh, Psammeticus I.

D.4. Names of additional biblical foreign warriors which derive from military terms

These names, like 'Goliath' have been regarded for generations as real names. When the Bible mentions kings and rules from Near Eastern countries, whether they be Judeans, Israelites or foreigners, it gives their exact or approximate names. This is attested to by many external documents such as the inscriptions that mention the House of David, and the House of Omri, Hezekiah, Mesha, Ben-Hadad and Hazael, Achish ben Padi, and the kings of Assyria, Babylon and Egypt. The Bible shortens long and complicated foreign names but they can be identified with their original ones. Shishak is Shoshenq, Necho is Nekau, Hophra is Wahibre Haaibre, Sennacherib is Sin-Ahhe-Erriba, Nebuchadnezzar is Nabu-kudurri-uszur, and so on. But there also seems to be a certain type of names in the Bible that define people by their epithets and not by their original personal names. This was when they were of a foreign origin, dangerous enemies of the people of Israel, of a high rank, warriors or outstanding heroes – whose real names were forgotten at the time of editing. The Bible gives their descriptions or epithets originating in the foreign language. In II Kings 18: 17 it is written: 'And the king of Assyria sent Tartan and Rabsaris and Rabshakeh'. These are descriptions of their positions in the Assyrian language (Tadmor 1983: 279-285. Ben Yosef Tawil 2010: 255, 267-268), but they lack the definite article and the impression is that these are personal names. In contrast to them, the ministers of Judah are mentioned both by name and title: 'And the king of Assyria sent Rabshakeh from Lachish to Jerusalem unto king Hezekiah … Then came forth unto him Eliakim, Hilkiah's son, which was over the house, and Shebna the scribe, and Joah, Asaph's son, the recorder. And Rabshakeh said unto them, Say ye now to Hezekiah … Then said Eliakim and Shebna and Joah unto Rabshakeh …' (Isaiah 36: 2-4, 11). There is a striking absence of the personal names in the stories about Joseph regarding the 'chief of the butlers' and the 'chief of the bakers' (Genesis 40: 2). However, the Babylonian ministers and commanders are mentioned by their titles and also their personal names: Nebuzaradan רַב-טַבָּחִים (the provost marshal, lit. chief cook) and Nebushasban רַב-סָרִיס (the chief attendant), Nergal Sharezer רַב-מָג (chief military official) (Jeremiah 39: 13) (Ben Yosef Tawil 2010: 355-356). This is because of the proximity of time and place, since their memory to the editors was still fresh and the Jews were then living in exile in Babylon.

It seems that to this type of name also belongs סִיסְרָא Sisra, the general of the army of Yavin, King of Hazor. In Chapters 4 and 5 of the Book of Judges, there is a description of a battle between the northern tribes of Israel and a coalition of Canaanite kings headed by Sisra. The first of these chapters is written in prose and the second one is the 'Song of Deborah'. The name Sisra has no meaning, and many researchers have tried to interpret it to learn of his identity. It is acceptable today that the name is non-Semitic. The wealth of assumptions raised about his origins extend over the entire Mediterranean. Noth thinks he is from Illyria in the Balkans, and that Sisra is one of the Sea Peoples (1960: 37, 150-151, 1602-1603). Lipinski assumes that the name is Anatolian and includes the widespread combinations in Anatolian names: Σεισα-/Σισα-/Ζιζα- together with -αρα (2006: 62). Garbini claims that Sisra is a Cretan and even identifies him with the Cretan god of the sky and storm, Zeus Cretagenes and with Dagon who was idolized in Gaza (1997: 179-182). What is common among these scholars is that they consider the name 'Sisra' as a personal name that came from the Sea Peoples over whom he was appointed. Zertal, the excavator of Tell al-Ahwat, explains in his book *Sisra's Secret* that the name reflects his origins in the region of Sassari in Sardinia (2010: 232-235). This suits his assumptions that the inhabitants of Tell al-Ahwat were Shardana, 'Sea Peoples' who had come from the island of Sardinia, and that this site should be identified with Sisra's place, חֲרֹשֶׁת הַגּוֹיִם Haroshet Hagoyim. But at the same time Zertal devotes a complete chapter in his book (Chapter 21, pp. 292-305) to the mystery of the Song of Deborah. Although it is listed among the most ancient texts in the Bible, the term 'אַדִּירִים' adirim (mighty, strong, noble, notable) which is frequently repeated in it - 'the people of the LORD came down to me against the mighty'; '…she brought forth butter in a lordly dish' (Judges 5: 13; 5:25) - is totally absent from the early books of the Bible. This term appears again only in late texts:

Jeremiah, Chronicles, Nehemia and Nahum. Zertal suggests as a solution that the 'אַדִּירִים' here were added in the later editing period, but prefers the possibility that 'סֵפֶל אַדִּירִים' sefel adirim (lordly dish) was taken from the Mycenaean world of experience to which the Sardinians belonged, in which it was the custom to greet the hero on his return home with a drink in special bowls. The Israelites on the other hand used to welcome their heroes with dance and song (Judges 11: 34; I Samuel 18: 6). Zertal finds a resemblance between the episode in which Yael offers Sisra a drink in a lordly dish and the episode in the Odyssey in which Nestor offers his guests a drink in an ornate golden cup (*Odyssey* XI: 618-641). This episode would have already been recognized throughout the Greek world in the 8th century BCE as is shown by the so-called *Nestor's cup* found in Pithekoussai on which there was an inscription in archaic Greek 'I am the cup of Nestor / from which it is good to drink ...' (Malkin 2003: 283-294). Zertal sums up that 'אַדִּירִים' is a literary reference to Shardana. A parallel term is 'עֲנָקִים' 'anakim (giants) which appears in the early books of the Bible (Numbers, Deuteronomy, Joshua, and Judges) and apparently originates in the Aegean word 'Anaku' which means 'ruler'. The expression 'lordly dish' is a remnant from the foreign culture that the Sardinians had brought with them (ibid: 305). In any case, Zertal has no solution for its appearance.

Zertal seems to indicate by his problem the possibility of resolving it by the fact that the expression 'lordly dish' was inserted during a later edition of the song. In Chapter 4, where there is a prose description of the battle and the death of Sisra, no mention is made of the 'lordly dish'. The description is a realistic one in which Yael opens the skin-bottle of milk and gives Sisra a drink from it. This is typical of the life conducted among the Kenite nomads in their tents, and is not an artificial borrowing from the life of nobles in their palaces and in their drinking parties. The word 'סֵפֶל' sefel is borrowed from the Akkadian word 'saplu', a cup made of bronze, or of copper or of gold (Ben Yosef Tawil 2010: 266). This type of cup appears, for example, in the biblical story of Joseph who hosts his brothers in his palace as the viceroy of the king of Egypt. There are various versions of the chapter because the Song of Deborah was meant to become a national epic. It was also meant to uplift and glorify Yael. Moreover, it was edited with the conscious awareness of the Homeric epic and in a polemical debate with the Aegean ethos and ideals of the army and its hero. There may also have been some dialogue with the tragedy Agammemnon of Aeschylus. Fleming Nielsen compares between the perception of tragedy in history in the writings of Herodotus and in the Bible. He assumes that Herodotus influenced Deut. historiography (1997: 160-164). If its final recension was in the Persian period, with the knowledge of the writing of Herodotus, it is reasonable to suppose that the works of Aeschylus were also known to the editor. Sisra, like Agammemnon, was the leading general of the coalition of kings, a champion in fighting with horses and chariots. Agammemnon returned home in a triumphal parade of chariots. His wife, Clytemnestra, a seeming ally like Yael, goes out to meet him with royal robes (like the mantle with which Yael covered Sisra). Agammemnon brings Cassandra and other captives with him, just as Sisra was supposed to have returned with '... to every man a damsel or two' (Judges 5: 30) רַחַם רַחֲמָתַיִם rakham rakhamatayim meaning captive women (a term also used in the Moabite inscription On Mesha Stele) with embroidered fabrics. His wife slays him with an ax. Cassandra also had the gift of prophecy granted her by Apollo, the sun god and the god of prophecy. But no one believed her (which recalls the lack of faith shown by Barak in the prophecy of Deborah). But while Cassandra foretold defeat to her people and death for her and Agammemnon, Deborah sang of victory and the revival of the people of Israel 'as the sun when he goeth forth in his might' (ibid. 5: 31).

In my opinion, the mystery of the dating for the term 'אַדִּירִים' is interwoven with the enigma of the name of Sisra. But instead of ascribing both of them to the period of the Sea Peoples, they should be regarded as additions made by a later recension. They were introduced into the Bible about the same time as the 'name' of Goliath. Even 'Sisra' is not a personal name but an epithet of Aegean martial origins: 'sis(t)ra' means συστράτηγος (the commander of joint armies). Συστρατιώτης is a fellow-warrior, a brother-in-arms. Συστρατεία means a joint military campaign (Herodotus VII.11); συστρατοπηδεύομαι means to live together in a common army camp. 'Συν' is the preposition that comes before the noun, adjective or verb. The last letter N/ν - 'νύ' is omitted if the first letter of the following word is a sigma σίγμα 'Σ/σ'. It has a number of meanings: a. To be together, in cooperation; b. To resemble; c. To take part in (Papanastasiou: 366-377). The adjective or epithet reflects the fact that Sisra was the commander of the joint forces of the kings of Canaan against the tribes of Israel.

The process of adoption undergone by the word συστράτηγος סִיסְטְרָאטֶגּוֹס in the Bible parallels the process of adoption for the word τύραννοι טִירָנוֹי. In both words the ταῦ (t) was dropped, and in the latter it turned into a samech (ך'׳סמ): seranim. In Greek the terms συστράτηγος, συστρατιώτης are late and do not appear in the Homeric epic, but only from the 5th century BCE in Herodotus, Euripides, and Xenophon. This means that in the Song of Deborah it was inserted in a later recension at about the time when the term אַדִּירִים was introduced, which appears in Jeremiah, Chronicles, Nehemiah and Nahum. But if the personal name of the commander of the Canaanite forces was forgotten, why did the Deut. author give him the Greek military title? Was it because Sisra was of Aegean origins, as was Goliath? Or perhaps for a similar reason as in the story of Goliath, to fight the Greeks with their own weapons?

There are scholars who assume that the name of Sisra indicates his origins from among the Sea Peoples, either from Anatolia or Sardinia. But if this was not his personal name but merely an epithet, in addition to the fact that it was attached to him in a much later period, it cannot be necessarily supposed. Moreover, the Bible is careful to note the ethnic origins of foreigners: Ephron the Hittite, Doeg the Edomite, Uriah the Hittite and Tselek the Ammonite, Ebed-melech the Kushite (apparently a Nubian). But Sisra was the commander of the armies of Canaanite kings, and nowhere has an ethnic label been attached to him that might suggest he was not a Canaanite. Confirmation for this can be found in I Samuel 12: 9-11: 'And when they forgot the Lord their God, he sold them into the hand of Sisra, captain of the host of Hazor, and into the hand of the Philistines, and into the hand of Moab, and they fought against them....And the Lord sent Jerubaal, and Bedan, and Jephthah, and Samuel, and delivered you out of the hand of your enemies on every side...'.Sisra of Canaanite Hazor is mentioned separately from the Philistines and Moab. Parallel with this, the names of the judges who fought against the different peoples are mentioned separately.

In Judges 4 it is told that Sisra lived in חֲרֹשֶׁת הַגּוֹיִם Haroshet hagoyim (lit. 'smithy of the foreign nations') where 900 chariots and horses were maintained. From the Song of Deborah it appears that the palace of Sisra was located there and it was the place where his mother and her servants lived. No place exists in Israel that retains the name and the traditions of this ancient site. Some scholars believe this was a city, and others that it was a complete region such as the Galilee. It is acceptable among most of them that it was a real place (see Zertal 2010: 236-246). But if 'Sisra' is a late Aegean title which means 'commander of the armies', perhaps the name 'Haroshet Hagoyim' is also a late epithet. A resemblance should be sought with στρατόπεδα, the fortified camps of the foreign mercenaries in the Egyptian Delta region. It seems that the ancient warrior and his military base for which the name and place has been forgotten were given Aegean characteristics appropriate to the realities of the time in which the story was composed. In the excavations of the massive fort in Tell el-Heir in Northern Sinai of the 6th century, which is identified with the mercenary settlement of Migdol, discovered among the Egyptian artifacts typical of the Saite dynasty, working tools, Phoenician storage jars, and many other vessels imported from the Greek islands, there was also a wealth of copper ore and dross (Oren 1992: 1111-1112). Perhaps they also served for arms production and craftsmanship.

The professional soldier and his heavy armor were sometimes held up to ridicule by the Greeks themselves. During the Peloponnesian Wars, Aristophanes portrayed the vainglorious warrior and soldier in his fullest stupidity and weakness. One of the targets for his arrows was Lamachus (Λάμαχος) the Athenian army commander from 435 to 415 BCE, who, like his name, was 'eager-for-war'. (Many Greek names were related to the army, war and victory, such as Telemachus, Callimachus, Stratonicus, Lysistratus). In the comedy *The Acharnians* Lamachus appears wearing armor and a helmet and complaining:

'εἰλιγγιῶ κάρα λίθῳ πεπληγμένος

σκοτοδινιῶ καὶ

...λόγχη τις ἐμπέπηγέ μοι δι' ὀστέων ὀδυρτά' (lines 1218-1220)

(This blow with the stone makes me dizzy; my sight grows dim...That spear has pierced my bones; what torture I endure!)

Also in his comedy *Peace* Aristophanes makes fun of Lamachus (vv. 1269-1293). After peace prevailed there was an attempt to use the helmets with crests for dusting tables and to turn armor into night pails. But even this was not attempted since the crests are losing all their hair and the armor 'pinches bottom' (vv. 1215-1239). Already in the 7th century BCE there was criticism of the ideal Homeric warrior in the words of the rebel poet Archilochus who preferred a short soldier with bandy but strong legs and a heart full of courage to a tall and bragging warrior (Frg. 114W in: Burnett, 43).

The comic element is also noticeable in the Sisra story, in the humoristic play on words: 'Sisra' and 'sur...sur...va'yasar' (Turn in... turn in to me; ... And he turned in unto her) (Judges 4: 18). And in his mother, waiting expectantly for his return, who boastfully speculates on the spoil that he will bring back. Here, too, the Bible uses its weapon of irony in its ideological battle with the Greek ethos. The supreme warrior, the chariot fighter, is defeated by the anti-hero, a nomadic woman living in a tent, and not even with a stone or rod which are a form of weapon as well, but with a 'workman's hammer'. Here as well deception and surprise are the decisive factor.

The Bible gives derogatory names to enemy commanders whose names were forgotten. These create a play on words and rhyming: Oreb and Zeeb (crow and wolf) the leaders of Midian, and Kushan-Rishathayim (Kushan double-wickedness) the king of Aram Naharayim (Judges 3: 8-9. 7:25). For the Philistine hero and the general of the Canaanite coalition, Greek names or epithets were chosen from the world of military terms that express power: 'armor' and 'military leader' that suited their external appearance and their assemblage of weapons. In Israel and in the Bible, the giving of names is of decisive importance. From Genesis it follows divine creation in which the name indicates goal and destiny. God changes the name of Abram to Abraham with whom he makes a covenant and appoints him to be the father of many nations, and he converts Jacob to Israel. It reflects circumstances, such as calling the name of Eli's grandson Ichabod (meaning dishonor) because he was born when the Philistines captured the Holy Ark. The name expresses a wish – Joseph ('God will increase'); character - Nimrod 'rebel', Peretz 'breach', and Naval whose wife Abigail testifies that he is like his name, a vile person. The Bible sometimes uses ironic names, such as the short-lived brothers מַחְלוֹן וְכִילְיוֹן Makhlon and Kilion (sickness and death), the sons of Naomi in the Book of Ruth. In the Bible we also find inverted speech in which a positive expression is used with a negative intention. For example, to 'bless' instead of to 'curse' (Job 2: 9: 'curse God and die'; I Kings 21:13: 'Naboth did blaspheme God and the king') This is also directed at the names of enemies defeated by unarmed Israelites who are technologically inferior. The irony is meant to be understood also by Greek listeners. The Greeks also used ironic names. The wise Titan Prometheus (foresighted), and his fool brother Epimetheus (lit. after-though). The latter married Pandora (all the gifts), who opened the box from which all the disasters of humankind emerged.

According to the Bible the Assyrians also used the language of their enemies for psychological warfare. Rabshakeh gave a speech in 'Judaean' to the besieged people in Jerusalem filled with threats and inducements so that they would surrender. The ministers of Hezekiah were well aware of the danger and requested Rabshakeh: 'Speak, I pray thee, to thy servants in the Syrian language [Aramaic]; for we understand it: and talk not with us in the Jews' language [Judaean] in the ears of the people on the wall'. The mocking answer of Rabshakeh exposes the aims of psychological warfare which are true for all times: 'Hath my master sent me to thy master, and to thee, to speak these words? hath he not sent me to the men which sit on the wall … Then Rabshakeh stood and cried with a loud voice in the Jews' language … Thus saith the king, Let not Hezekiah deceive you: for he shall not be able to deliver you out of his hand' (II Kings 18: 26-29). He even used their own religious faith to undermine their confidence, saying that God was angry with them because Hezekiah had centered the cult in Jerusalem: 'But if ye say unto me, We trust in the Lord our God; is not that he whose high places and whose altars Hezekiah hath taken away, and hath said to Judah and Jerusalem, Ye shall worship before this altar in Jerusalem?' (ibid. 22). Sennacherib claims to be the messenger of God who is angry at them and an instrument to punish them: 'Am I now come up without the Lord against this place to destroy it? The Lord said to me, Go up against this land, and destroy it' (ibid. 25). Cyrus also claimed that the Gods of Babylon destroyed it because of their anger at the cultic reforms of Nabonides, and that he himself was sent by Marduk, their chief god, to subdue it. (http://www.britishmuseum.org/research/search_the_collection_database/search_object_details.aspx?objectid=327188&partid=1). The words of Rabshakeh reflect, in a distorted mirror, the rebuke of Isaiah: 'O Assyrian, the rod of mine anger, and the staff in their hand is mine indignation. I will send him against an hypocritical nation, and against the people of my wrath will I give him a charge, to take the spoil, and to take the prey, and to tread them down like the mire in the streets… Shall I not, as I have done in Samaria and her idols, so do to Jerusalem and her idols?' (Isaiah 10: 5-11). Of course, in Isaiah the punishment is not for removing the high places but on the contrary, for the continued worship of idols in Jerusalem in spite of all Hezekiah's efforts.

E. Who was the enemy represented by Goliath? The Saites and their Aegean mercenaries

The use of Greek names are a confirmation of the thesis of Yadin that the Bible is warring against the Greeks, against their ethos and their literature by using their own weapons. But it is still necessary to clarify the difficulties posed against this by Heard who asks: What is the logic in warring against the Greeks in particular, when the enemies at that time were mainly Babylon and to a lesser extent Egypt? And how can a 'national epic' end in the destruction of the kingdom and in exile?

To answer this, it is necessary to examine how the Bible views Babylon and Egypt at the time when the story was edited. They were responsible for the destruction of Judah, the former directly and the latter indirectly. Both of them took in the Jewish people who had been exiled from their country, and the attitude of the Bible towards the Jewish communities that took form in Babylon and Egypt should be clarified.

In the eyes of the biblical author, Babylon was not the enemy that the Jews should have warred against. Jeremiah and Ezekiel stressed that they should have accepted their superiority and rule since this was the instrument of punishment by God against sinful Judah and its neighbors (Jeremiah 46: 16; 50: 16; Ezekiel 29-30; 32: 11). God calls Nebuchadnezzar 'my servant' (Jeremiah 25: 9; 27: 6; 43: 10), whose task was: 'Thou art my battle-ax and weapons of war; for with thee will I break in pieces the nations, and with thee will I destroy kingdoms' (Jeremiah 51: 20). At the same time, Isaiah, Habbakuk and Jeremiah foretold also the destruction of Babylon after it had accomplished this task. The destruction of Babylon is of central importance in the prophecies of Jeremiah (Hoffman 2001: 826-830). He publicly opposed the revolt, and even during the siege of Jerusalem he announced that all those who fell captive to the Chaldeans would be save. He himself tried to escape from the city, was accused as a traitor by the pro-Egyptian party, was cast into a dungeon, where he was sunk into the mire. But secretly, in the fourth year of Zedekiah, he commands Seraiah the son of Neriah (brother of Baruch) to take the book of his prophecies of destruction to Babylon: 'Then shalt thou say, O Lord, thou has spoken against this place, to cut it off, that none shall remain in it, neither man nor beast, but that it shall be desolate forever. And it shall be, when thou has made an end of reading this book, that thou shalt bind a stone to it, and cast it into the midst of the Euphrates. And thou shalt say, Thus shall Babylon sink, and shall not rise from the evil that I shall bring upon her' (Jeremiah 51: 62-64). The secrecy was not due to fears for his life, since even in the shadow of death he did not cease to express his views in the courts of Jehoiakim and Zedekiah. He even stood in the entrance to the palace of Pharaoh Apries in Egypt and prophesied his destruction (see below); But matters should not be precipitated, until Babylon had accomplished its mission for Judah and her neighbors. It appears that his caution was also the result of his wish to prevent persecution and repression of the exiles in Babylon. Moreover, in the letter he sent by a member of the delegation of Zedekiah to Babylon, Jeremiah instructed the exiles who were with Jehoiachin to adapt themselves and settle in their surroundings in order to survive and be able to return to their homeland (see Sections F.2 and G): 'And seek the peace of the city whither I have caused you to be carried away captives, and pray unto the Lord for it: for in the peace thereof shall ye have peace. For thus saith the Lord of hosts, the God of Israel: Let not your prophets and your diviners, that be in the midst of you, deceive you, neither hearken to your dreams which ye cause to be dreamed. For they prophesy falsely unto you in my name: I have not sent them, saith the Lord' (Jeremiah 29: 7-9). The prophets who incited violent opposition to Babylon, were indeed executed by Nebuchadnezzar (ibid. 21-22). Also Ezekiel, one of the leaders of those exiled with Jehoiachin, refrained from preaching against Babylon.

Why then should Babylon be destroyed? Firstly, as punishment for its arrogance. Nebuchadnezzar aspires to resolve the fate of nations. Therefore: 'How is the hammer of the whole earth cut asunder and broken! How is Babylon become a desolation among the nations! I have laid a snare for thee, and thou art also taken, O Babylon ... thou art found and also caught, because thou has striven against the Lord' (Jeremiah 50: 23-24). Its fate was like that of the Assyrian king of whom Isaiah had prophesied: 'Wherefore it shall come to pass, that when the Lord hath performed his whole work upon mount Zion and on Jerusalem, I will punish the fruit of the stout heart of the king of Assyria, and the glory of his high looks. For he saith, By the strength of my hand I have done it, and by my wisdom; for I am prudent: and I have removed the bounds of the people, and have robbed their treasures, and I have put down the inhabitants like a valiant man. ...Shall the ax boast itself against him that heweth therewith? Or shall the saw magnify itself against him that shaketh it?' (Isaiah 10: 12-5). Its destruction will also prove the superiority of God over its idols: 'A sword in upon the Chaldeans,... for it is the land of graven images, and they are made upon their idols' (Jeremiah 50: 35-38). '...say Babylon is taken, Bel is confounded, Merodach is broken in pieces; her idols are confounded' (ibid. 50: 2). The Second Isaiah envisioned a procession of idols led in captivity: 'Bel boweth down, Nebo stoopeth, their idols were upon the beasts, and upon the cattle: your carriages were heavy loaden; they are a burden to the weary beast. They stoop, they bow down together; they could not deliver the burden, but themselves are gone into captivity' (Isaiah 46: 1-2). In the Bible, Babylon symbolizes the evil: 'Behold I am against thee, O thou most evil ... for thy day is come, the time that I will visit thee. And the most evil shall stumble and fall, and none shall raise him up' (Jeremiah 50: 31-32). The memory of her cruelty towards Judah and the desire for revenge remained among the exiles in spite of the need to adapt and survive: 'O daughter of Babylon, who art to be destroyed; happy shall he be that rewardeth thee as thou has served us. Happy shall he be that taketh and dasheth thy little ones against the stones' (Psalms 137: 8-9). 'And I will render unto Babylon and to all the inhabitants of Chaldea all their evil that they have done in Zion in your sight' (Jeremiah 51: 24). Babylon became the symbol of hubris and evil in the Bible and its punishment is combined with the salvation of the Jewish people (Hoffman 2004:20-28). God will destroy her prison when he comes to liberate the exiles and return them to Zion: 'The children of Israel and the children of Judah were oppressed together: and all that took them captive held them fast; they refused to let them go. ... A sword is upon... the inhabitants of Babylon... and it shall be no more inhabited forever: neither shall it be dwelt in from generation to generation' (ibid. 50: 33-39).

Babylon, whose end was certain and the exiles would return from it to their land, would not therefore be a danger to the Jewish people. The attitude of the Bible to Egypt is different and complex. On one hand there is no hatred for the Egyptian people. Since the days of Abraham they found food and lodging there in times of crisis. But when they increased in numbers, the Pharaoh turned them into slaves, and even decreed their partial destruction. But Israel was commanded: '…thou shalt not abhor an Egyptian because thou wast a stranger in his land. The children that are begotten of them shall enter into the congregation of the Lord in their third generation' (Deuteronomy 23: 7-8). Joseph also married Osnat, the daughter of Potiphar, Priest of On, and their children – Ephraim and Menashe – were the largest among the tribes of Israel. On the other hand, the Bible severely attacks the gods of Egypt – and also its Saitic rulers and their mercenaries who supported their regime. Towards the end of the kingdom of Judah, this was expressed by Jeremiah and Ezekiel: 'Behold, I will punish the [god Amon] of Nō, and Pharaoh and Egypt with their gods and their kings; even Pharaoh and all them that trust in him' (Jeremiah 46: 25). And Ezekiel says: 'Thus saith the Lord God; Behold I am against thee, Pharaoh king of Egypt, the great dragon that lieth in the midst of his rivers, which hath said, My river is mine own, and I have made it for myself. But I will put hooks into thy jaws ….and I will bring them up out of the midst of thy rivers, and all the fish of thy rivers shall stick unto thy scales. And I will leave thee thrown into the wilderness … for meat to the beasts of the field and to the fowls of the heaven. And all the inhabitants of Egypt shall know that I am the Lord' (Ezekiel 29:3-6). Pharaoh was considered a god in Egypt and was identified with the crocodile god Sobek, the creator of the Nile that fertilized the whole country. The image of the crocodile is included in the hieroglyph of sovereign and Pharaoh exterminating his enemies is compared to him. In the Bible, on the other hand, the crocodile – תַּנִּין tannin is called רַהַב rahav (*hybris*), who rebelled against God and was punished. God himself fights the crocodile-Pharaoh, and fishes him out of his river. He will scourge him with his own hands as well as the other gods of Egypt, and in all the cities where their cultic centers were found. This was in contrast with Babylon, where God will watch from the side its destruction and the collapse of its gods. The instrument of punishment against Egypt would be Nebuchadnezzar, who would invade it: 'Behold, I will send and take Nebuchadrezzar the king of Babylon, my servant … And when he cometh, he shall smite the land of Egypt… And I will kindle a fire in the houses of the gods of Egypt; and he shall burn them, and carry them away captives… He shall also break the images of Beth-shemesh that is in the land of Egypt; and the houses of the gods of the Egyptians shall he burn with fire' (Jeremiah 43: 10-13). 'Beth-shemesh' (in Hebrew, 'the house of the sun') is On (Heliopolis), the center of the cult for the sun god Atum-Ra. This would be the fate of the city of the chief god Amun, which was called נֹא אָמוֹן Nō-Amon (Thebes) in Upper Egypt: 'Behold I will punish the multitude of Nō, and Pharaoh, and Egypt, with their gods, and their kings: even Pharaoh and them that trust in him (Jeremiah 46: 25). Ezekiel also describes the conquest of Egypt by Nebuchadnezzar, during which God himself would destroy the cities of Egypt and its gods: 'And I will make Pathros desolate, and will set fire in Zoan, and will execute judgments in Nō. And I will pour my fury upon Sin, the strength of Egypt; and I will cut off the multitude of Nō. And I will set fire in Egypt; Sin shall have great pain, and Nō shall be rent asunder, and Noph shall have distresses daily' (Ezekiel 30: 14-16). 'Sin' is Syene/Swene (Aswan) on the Nubian border, and 'Noph' is Moph (Memphis).

Egypt will be destroyed also as punishment for the Pharaos policy towards Judah: '… because they have been a staff of reeds to the house of Israel… when they leaned upon thee, thou brakest … And the land of Egypt shall be desolate and waste; and they shall know that I am the Lord' (Ezekiel 29: 6-9). At the beginning of the First Temple period Egypt was too weak to impose its control over Israel and Judah, but tried to bring them under its influence in its struggle against the Mesopotamian powers. In the 8th century the kings of Israel turned to it in the hope of gaining its assistance against the Assyrian threat. The prophets regarded the alliance with it as leading to catastrophe because of its weakness and treachery. Hosea opposed the double game played by the kings of Israel: 'Ephraim is like a silly dove without heart, they call to Egypt, they go to Assyria' (Hosea 7: 11); 'Ephraim feedeth on wind, and followeth after the east wind: he daily increases lies and desolation; and they do make a covenant with the Assyrians, and oil is carried into Egypt' (ibid. 12:2). Hoshea, king of Israel sought the help of So (Sais, the capital of the Egyptian Pharaoh) against Shalmaneser, king of Assyria, but in vain. Samaria was besieged (II Kings 17: 6-20) and was destroyed in 720 BCE by Sargon II. Isaiah was opposed to the reliance on Egypt: 'Woe to the rebellious children…. That walk to go down into Egypt, and have not asked at my mouth; to strengthen themselves in the strength of Pharaoh, and to trust the shadow of Egypt! Therefore shall the strength of Pharaoh be your shame, and the trust in the shadow of Egypt your confusion … For the Egyptians shall help in vain, and to no purpose' (Isaiah 30: 1-7). Egypt came under the rule of Assyria during the reign of Esarhaddon (681-668 BCE) and Ashurbanipal (689-627 BCE). They appointed Necho I (672-664 BCE) of Sais as the governor on their behalf. His son, Psammeticus I (664-610 BCE) recruited thousands of mercenaries from Asia Minor, and with their help he revolted against Assyria and united Egypt under his rule.

In the 7th-6th centuries BCE the professional foreign army was the central pillar of support for the Saite rulers, and they depended on it to suppress all opposition at home as well as in their wars with the Assyrians, Nubians and Babylonians. Assyria became mired in internal warfare after the death of Ashurbanipal and was greatly weakened. Josiah took advantage of this to conduct cultic reforms in his kingdom and apparently aspired to extend its boundaries once again after it had been narrowed by Sennacherib. But the Saites subverted this by gaining power Philistia and Judah. This was of great strategic and economic importance to them. The 'sea route' passed through this territory in which since earliest times the Egyptians had conducted their military campaigns against their enemies in the north. The port cities along the coast were of strategic importance, and they also brought enormous profit from international trade. Psammeticus besieged Ashdod for twenty-nine years until he conquered it, and Necho conquered Gaza. In the Ashqelon excavations Ionic pottery of the 7th century and the beginning of the 6th century BCE was found. Fantalkin thinks this was not the result of trade with Greece, or that there were Greek traders living there, but that it belonged to the Aegean garrison in the service of Egypt.[22] A pottery fragment found in the excavations, with the inscription εμι ατατο (I am

---

[22] In the view of Fantalkin, the statement in Herodotus that Naukratis was 'once' the only trading port in Egypt (II.179) refers to the period before the reign of Amasis in 570 BCE, when Greek traders were not allowed to operate along the Israelite and the southern Phoenician coast, but only in Naukratis in Egypt. Amasis was the first to open additional ports for trade with Greece (Fantalkin 2008: 286-291). Recently, the port of Thonis-Heraklion was discovered at the end of the Canopic branch of the Nile Delta where it flows into the Mediterranean Sea. It appears that this was the first station of the traders on their way to Naukratis as indicate

of Atatos) (Cross 2006: 367) can confirm this. This is because the name, which means 'insatiable' suits a mercenary, as it is the epithet for Ares the god of war in the Iliad (V: 388) (Fantalkin 2009). Aegean mercenaries in the service of Egypt also occupied the Mesad Hashavyahu fort in Judah, which was in operation from 620 to 605 BCE. Found in it were large quantities of ceramics in the 'wild goat' style which comes from Asia Minor and the Aegean islands in the 7th-6th centuries BCE. Alongside this, *ostraca* were discovered with Hebrew inscriptions. One of them, called the 'harvester letter' shows that Judaean farmers cultivated the nearby fields for the governor of the fort and suffered persecution and injustice (Naveh 1961: 119-128). In the opinion of Fantalkin, the fort was built by the Saites in order to protect the port of Yavne-Yam and to serve as a logistic base in their campaigns to the north. Tell Kabri was also a fort in which Aegean mercenaries were stationed. Niemeier thinks they were in the service of Tyre (2001: 15-17); Fantalkin believes they served Egypt (2008: 269-274, 280-284). He explains the brief period in the existence of Ionic pottery throughout the country by the correlation he found between the years of Egyptian rule, from the last two decades of the 7th century BCE until the Babylonian conquest. He claims that the Greek mercenaries only served the Egyptian army. This is because in the southern Levant hardly any Greek pottery has been found during the periods of Assyrian and Babylonian rule, and only during the 20-25 years of its conquest by the Saites (Fantalkin 2006: 201-205; Idem 2008: 199-207).

However, there does exist evidences for the hiring of Greek mercenaries in Assyria such as the identical bronze horse frontlets and blinkers of horses that were captured in 732 BCE from the palace of Hazael in Damascus and that were discovered in sanctuaries throughout Greece. They seem to have been pieces of armor looted from the enemy and dedicated as a thanksgiving offering for the victory by the mercenaries in the army of Tiglath-Pileser III. Another evidence is the famous Phoenician silver bowl from Amathus, Cyprus, that was fashioned between 710 and 675 BCE, which describes Assyrians with hoplites laying siege against a city, while archers and other Greek hoplites defended it (Niemeier 2001: 14-15, 21; Luraghi 2006: 33-40) **(Fig. 14)**. In my opinion there is another proof. In the reliefs found in Sennacherib's palace in Nineveh that describe the siege of Lachish in Judah in the year 701 BCE by the Assyrian army, some of the soldiers have large round shields, greaves, and high crested helmets with cheek guards which differed from the armor and conical helmets of the other soldiers **(Fig. 15)**. In the excavations of Lachish III (during the siege period) a fragment of a bronze helmet of this kind was found (Ussishkin 1981: 55-80). The helmets are identical in all their details to the famous bronze helmet of the end of the 8th century BCE which is held in the archaeological museum of Argos (ANC277226) **(Fig. 4)**. Esarhaddon also employed Cilician and Greek mercenaries and assumed the throne in 681 BCE with their assistance (Raaflaub 2004: 207-208). Mercenaries from Caria and Ionia suppressed rebellions in Egypt against Necho I and Psammeticus I during the Assyrian conquest (Herodotus II.151; Polyaenus 7: 3) (see Section F.1). Mercenaries were also hired by Babylon such as Antimenidas. As

---

the steles of tax officials beginning from the reign of Psammeticus II (595-589 BCE), as well as Eastern Greek pottery of the second half of the 6th century BCE. From the taxation laws that were inscribed on steles from the reign of Nekhtnebef I (380-362 BCE) of the 30th dynasty in Naukratis and Thonis-Heraklion, about 10% of the import taxes that came from the 'seas of the Greeks' as well as the production taxes in Naukratis were dedicated to Neith in Sais. Apparently these laws had existed since the days of the Saite rulers (Villing & Schlotzhauer 2006: 5 and notes 20-22).

Fig. 14. Silver Phoenician bowl.
Date: 750-600 BCE. Made in Phoenicia or Cyprus. Findspot: Tomb at Amathus, Limassol district, Cyprus. The British Museum, No. 123053. © The Trustees of the British Museum.
The bowl was found in a copper cauldron along with an iron dagger and the fragments of a shield. Fragmentary; decorated in repoussée and engraved figures and motifs; in the center is a rosette medallion surrounded by three concentric registers of figures. Outer scene shows the siege of a city with files of military figures wearing hoplite, Egyptian and Urartian gear with fragmentary chariot entering from right side.

FIG. 15. ASSYRIAN SOLDIER WITH HOPLITE GEAR.
GYPSUM WALL PANEL RELIEF FROM SENNACHERIB PALACE. DATE: 704-681 BCE (CIRCA).
FINDSPOT: SOUTH WEST PALACE, NINEVEH (KOUYUNJIK), IRAQ. THE BRITISH MUSEUM, NO.
124950. © The Trustees of the British Museum.
THE UPPER PART OF A SOLDIER IN THE KING'S RETINUE, LOOKING TO LEFT, WEARING AEGEAN
HELMET WITH CURVED HIGH CREST AND CARRYING A ROUND SHIELD AND SPEAR.

said above, they were recruited together with their φίλοι and ξένοι (see also Section F.2). The prophet Ezekiel relates that the soldiers of Nebuchadnezzar did not receive wages for his war against Tyre, and therefore he will conquer Egypt and plunder it in order to pay them their due. From the Bible and archaeological evidence it appears that also the kings of Judah hired Aegean mercenaries, and scores of mercenaries served in the citadel of Arad.[23]

Babylon became empowered during the reign of Nabopolassar (626-605 BCE) and Nebuchadnezzar (605-562 BCE), and Necho II tried to halt its expansion. In 609 BCE he went to Carchemish near the Euphrates to help Ashur-uballit II, king of Assyria, who was fighting against Nebuchadnezzar, but was defeated. In excavations at Carchemish, scarabs of Necho were found near hoplite armor and weapons of Aegean mercenaries (Niemeier 2001: 20-23). On his way northwards he killed Josiah who had gone to confront him in Megiddo. On the way back he took Jehoahaz the son of Josiah as a hostage to Egypt, and crowned Jehoiakim in his place. Jeremiah and his companions became disillusioned with the dream of Judah's political greatness and understood that it was only a plaything in the hands of Egypt and Babylon, and that Babylon had become the decisive power in the region. But the later kings of Judah did not interpret correctly the often changing balance of power between these two world powers. Nebuchadnezzar conquered the Hittite kingdom, and in 604 BCE conducted a campaign against Ashqelon. He subdued Jehoiakim who had rebelled against him after three years of servitude (II Kings 24: 2-3). During the siege that the Babylonians imposed on Jerusalem, Jehoiakim died. His son and heir, Jehoiachin, surrendered in 597 BCE and was exiled to Babylon with the ruling and economic elite of Judah. Nebuchadnezzar crowned Zedekiah who swore fealty to him. In 601 BCE Nebuchadnezzar conducted a military campaign against Egypt, but was repulsed by Necho, and during the first decade of the 6th century his rule was weakened

---

[23] The Bible ascribes to David the hiring of the 'Cherethites and Pelethites', as well as six hundred Philistine warriors from Gath (II Samuel 15: 18). In II Samuel 20: 23 it says the 'הכרי והפלתי' (the Carians and Pelethites) and this version is indeed appropriate to the real situation during the period of the Deut. recension. But also in earlier periods the kings of Judah employed Carian mercenaries (II Kings 11: 4). Cretan mercenaries also appeared in the area around 700 BCE. At that time an economic crisis occurred in Crete which caused a large emigration from there. The Homeric epic that was composed in its final form around 700 BCE describes the Cretans dealing in trade and sea piracy. Odysseus disguised himself as a Cretan and relates how he with his companions invaded the coast of Egypt, was defeated, and was taken into service by the king of Egypt (*Odyssey* XIV: 199-298). From excavations in the citadel of Arad it appears that 'Kittim' mercenaries occupied it around the year 600, and ostraca were found written in Hebrew that order food supplies for them. According to Aharoni (1968: 103) and Finkelstein (2003: 337-339) they were in the service of Judah. In contrast to their view, Na'aman (1991: 47-48) believes they were in the service of Egypt that had then extended its rule over Judah. Fantalkin thinks that the 'Cherethites and Pelethites' in David's stories reflect the Carian mercenaries of Egypt in the late 7th century BCE (2008: 350-368, 430). However, even if the Kittim wore scale armor as was the practice in their country, it is no reasonable to identify them with Goliath, the enemy of David, Israel and its God. This also applies to the Carian mercenaries of Judah who restored Joash of the Davidic dynasty to the throne and expelled Athaliah, the usurper queen. Moreover, they acted in accordance with the order of God. Jehoiada the High Priest brought them into the Temple, made a covenant with them and appointed them as bodyguards for Joash (II Kings: 12). He even armed them with the spears and shields of King David that were kept in the Temple. However, the Book of Chronicles omits any mention of the Carians in this event. On the contrary, stress was laid on the prohibition to enter the Temple which applied even to the Jewish participants: 'But let none come into the house of the Lord, save the priests and they that minister of the Levites; they shall go in, for they are holy' (II Chronicles 23: 6). It was the Levites and not the Carians who were appointed as bodyguards for Joash. Jehoiada gave the conspirators 'the spears and bucklers and shields that had been King David's which were in the house of God' (ibid. 6-9). The book of Chronicles was written during the Persian period, when the isolation from the gentiles was of supreme importance for the spiritual leadership.

because of internal upheavals. On the other hand, the Egyptian Pharaoh Psammeticus II (601-589 BCE) succeeded in overcoming Nubia and even conducted a campaign to demonstrate his power to the land of 'kharu' (Canaan and Phoenicia). All this caused a complete reversal in the foreign policy of Zedekiah, who violated his vow of loyalty to Babylon (Wiseman 1991: 36; Kahn 2008: 139-153). He rebelled during the first year of Pharaoh Apries (589-570 BCE) who also promised him aid. But in the eyes of Jeremiah and Ezekiel the alliance with the Saites was considered atrocious. They had killed Joshiah, their esteemed king and forced upon the people the compliant Jehoiakim, an idol worshipper who did violent deeds and shed innocent blood until Jeremiah prophesied for him 'the burial of an ass' (Jeremiah 22: 19). Their incitement to rebel against Babylon was disastrous. Among the people the propaganda for revolt was spread by false prophets, such Hananiah the son of Azur who broke the yoke that Jeremiah carried on his neck in token of the subjection of Judah the neighboring countries to Nebuchadnezzar, saying: 'Even so will I break the yoke of Nebuchadnezzar, king of Babylon from the neck of all nations' (Jeremiah 28: 11). Ezekiel also compared Apries to a rickety wall on which Judah is plastering with fake mortar: 'So will I break down the wall that ye have daubed with untempered mortar and bring it down to the ground, so that the foundation thereof shall be discovered, and it shall fall and ye shall be consumed in the midst thereof' (Ezekiel 13: 14). The Egyptian relief force sent a year after the beginning of the siege of Jerusalem was of no help. The Babylonians retreated for a while, but returned to renew the siege until the city was conquered (Jeremiah 37-39).

It was especially Apries who aroused the anger of the prophets because he aggrandized his image with the powers of creation: 'My river is mine own, and I have made it for myself' (Ezekiel 29: 3). They derided his military impotence and lack of trustworthiness. Redford and Freedy showed that the prophecy of Ezekiel (30:20-24) who repeats the assurance four times that God will break the Pharoe's arms, 'both the strong arm and the one that was broken', is an ironic play on his Nebty name, Nb ḫpš, which means 'Possessor of strong arm'. Also his father, Psammeticus II attached the term 'strong arms' to his name, and in their documents the Saites ascribed their victories to the power of their arms (1970: 482-483). Shupak studied the influence of Egyptian wisdom literature in the Bible. She believes that it had already begun in the days of Solomon who married the daughter of Pharaoh (1993: 353-354). The ideal wise man in Egypt was the 'gr', the reserved and silent person. His opposite was the talkative and noisy fool. Also in the Book of Proverbs (ascribed to Solomon): 'Even a fool, when he holdeth his peace, is counted wise; and he that shutteth his lips is esteemed a man of understanding' (Proverbs 17: 28). The personalization of Wisdom in the book resembles the Egyptian goddess Ma'at (ibid: 345-346). The cultural influence of Egypt on Judah and Philistia strengthened in the 7th century BCE when they became her vassals and paid tax to her. There is a considerable amount of archaeological evidence for this (see the review of them in Shipper 2011: 274-279). Hoffmeier noted that Jeremiah (46: 17) by saying that Pharaoh was called שָׁאוֹן shaon (noise, tumult), indicates his stupidity, in contrast with the 'gr' ideal. By the other epithet as well 'הֶעֱבִיר הַמּוֹעֵד' heebhir ha'moed (meaning: he has passed the time appointed, missed his opportunity) there is a play on words with his Egyptian name ה-היב-רע h"ibr' (1981: 167-168. 1997: 159). He is a bragger like Sisra and Goliath and his military and technological power is worthless as theirs because God himself is warring against him.

Herodotus also describes Apries as arrogant, stupid and without military talent. He sent the Egyptian army against the Greek colony of Cyrene which was defeated and nearly totally decimated, and his Egyptian subjects claimed that he was trying to eliminate them in order to ensure his rule. His cruelty even towards his loyal ministers caused his people to revolt against him. He fought them with the help of 30,000 mercenaries from Caria and Ionia (Herodotus II.163; Diodorus I.68.2-5). Even after their downfall, he was sure that no god could depose him from his throne (Herodotus II.166).

According to Egyptian historiography, during the period of Sethon, high priest of Ptah and ruler of Memphis, Egypt was delivered from the conquest of Sennacherib by mice who gnawed at night the weapons of his army (Herodotus II.141). It is very similar to the biblical story in which Judah is saved from conquest by Sennacherib after an angel smote 185,000 of his soldiers (II Kings 19: 35). Moreover, the Bible also drew much from Egyptian theology. The very 'birth certificate' of Deut. history, the story about the discovery of the Mosaic law book by Josiah during the Temple repairs and the motivation it gave to conduct cultic reforms, was copied from an Egyptian religious formula created a hundred years earlier. The king, Shabaka (716-701 BCE) of the 25th 'Nubian' dynasty, relates in an inscription engraved on a basalt stone known as the Shabaka Stone, that during repairs to the Temple of Ptah in Memphis he found a worm-eaten papyrus. He commanded that what was written on it, the main principles of Memphis theology, should be engraved on stone. In the wake of this discovery, a cultic reform was conducted that designated Ptah, the god of wisdom and craftsmanship, as the main god of Memphis and placed him at the center of the universe as its creator. There is a debate as to whether the inscription is really the copy of an original ancient text composed about 2000 years earlier (Wilson, in *ANET*, Pritchard 1950: 4-6) or merely pretending to be ancient, and was actually composed in the political interests of Shabaka in order to gain the support of the Ptah priests by enhancing their status. (http://www.britishmuseum.org/explore/highlights/highlight_objects/aes/t/the_shabako_stone.aspx).

Whether this or the other, the story that established monotheism in Judaism was taken from Egyptian pagan worship, 'judaized' and used as a weapon against idolatry itself. The prophets, in their struggle against the Saites, also used Egyptian names, terms and literary values as well as Saite military ideals. Their psychological warfare was not extended only outwards but also inwardly to persuade those Judaeans who believed that Egypt would save them from the hand of Babylon.

The hostility towards the Aegean mercenaries and the attempts to belittle their image in the stories of Sisra and Goliath are understandable in view of their participation in the conquest and destruction of the Land of Israel and in exiling its inhabitants in the 7th and 6th centuries BCE. They had manned the fortresses of the Egyptian government and supervision over the local population, and represented the foreign and oppressive regime. The prophets generally addressed the ruler or his country and people. However, in an extraordinary address to the mercenaries of Pharaoh, Jeremiah describes their defeat, firstly in the Battle of Carchemish: 'The word of the Lord which came to Jeremiah .... Against the army of Pharaoh Necho king of Egypt ...in Carchemish, which Nebuchadrezzar king of Babylon smote ... Order ye the buckler and the shield, and draw near to battle. Harness the horses; and get up ye horsemen, and stand forth with your helmets; furbish the spears, and put on the brigandines ... For this is the day of the Lord God of hosts, a day of vengeance that he may avenge him of his adversaries; and the sword shall devour, and it shall be satiate and made drunk with their blood: for the Lord God of hosts hath a sacrifice in the north country by the river Euphrates... for the mighty man hath stumbled against the mighty, and they are fallen both together' (Jeremiah 46: 1-12).

Jeremiah also prophesies defeat to the mercenaries of Apries when Nebuchadnezzar invades Egypt: 'Declare ye in Egypt and publish in Migdol, and publish in Noph and Tahpanhes; ... Why are thy valiant men swept away? they stood not, because the Lord did drive them. He made many to fall, yea one fell upon another; and they said, Arise, and let us go again to our own people, and to the land of our nativity, from the oppressing sword ... They did cry there, Pharaoh king of Egypt is but a noise; he hath passed the time appointed' (ibid. 14-17). Jeremiah gloats over the mercenaries and stresses the worthlessness of the helmets, armors and shields that became impediments that caused them to fall upon each other. The terrified hoplites want to desert Egypt and return to their homeland, just like the defeated Aegean mercenaries of Cyrus II (the Younger), two hundred years later, described by Xenophon in his *Anabasis*. Jeremiah stresses the relationship between Egypt and the Aegean mercenaries by comparing both of them to heifers: 'Egypt is like a very fair heifer ... Also her hired men are in the midst of her like fatted bullocks; for they also are turned back and are fled away together; they did not stand' (ibid. 20-21). The goddess Neith, founder and patron of Sais, is portrayed in the form of a cow. The cow statue that stood in the royal palace in Sais was tomb and also the incarnation of Pharaoh's daughter Men-Kau-Ra/Μυκερινος (Herodotus II.129-132). Jeremiah prayed that after the defeat of the mercenaries the rule of the Saites in Egypt would collapse: 'The daughter of Egypt shall be confounded; she shall be delivered into the hand of the people of the north. ...Behold I will punish the [god Amon] of Nō, and Pharaoh and Egypt with their gods, and their kings; even Pharaoh and all them that trust in him. And I will deliver them into the hand of those that seek their lives, and into the hand of Nebuchadrezzar king of Babylon and into the hands of his servants; and afterward it shall be inhabited as in the days of old' (46: 24-26). Jeremiah also predicts the end of the Saites when he arrives in Egypt with the remnants of Judah. In a symbolic act, he buries large stones in the entrance to the palace of Apries in Tahpanhes as a platform for the throne of Nebuchadnezzar who would come in the future as a conqueror (ibid. 43: 8-13). He prophesies that: 'Behold, I will give Pharaoh-hophra king of Egypt into the hand of his enemies, and into the hands of them that seek his life; as I gave Zedekiah king of Judah into the hand of Nebuchadnezzar king of Babylon, his enemy, and that sought his life' (ibid. 44: 30). Ezekiel also separates the fate of Egypt from the fate of her rulers. The land would be conquered and destroyed and its people would be dispersed among the nations for forty years, but the nation would return and be rehabilitated, although it would never regain its former power. It would nevermore cause Israel to sin, and would recognize the greatness of God: 'And it shall be no more the confidence of the house of Israel, which bringeth their iniquity to remembrance, when they shall look after them; but they shall know that I am the Lord God' (Ezekiel 29: 8-16).

In the description of the mercenaries, there are many similarities between 'for the battle is the Lord's' against Goliath and the God that fights the mercenaries himself. Even against Sisra: 'They fought from heaven; the stars in their courses fought against Sisra' (Judges 5: 20). Compare Goliath who curses God with 'for this is the day of vengeance for the Lord to avenge himself against his enemies', and between Goliath the giant who was struck and fell and the stuffed hoplite that God strikes and fells. There is even an opposed parallel between the elegy of David after the defeat of Israel by the Philistines (II Samuel 1: 19-27) and the song of triumph and revenge against the mercenaries: 'Tell it not in Gath, publish it not in the streets of Ashqelon' as compared with 'Declare ye in Egypt and publish in Migdol, and publish in Noph and Tahpanhes', and 'How are the mighty fallen, and the weapons of war perished', as against 'for the mighty man hath stumbled against the mighty, and they are fallen both together'.

What is the significance of the similarities between the descriptions, and what is the connection between the story of Goliath the Philistine and the prophecies of Jeremiah about the hoplites? The answer lies in a subject that has not been dealt with in research until now: the myth of the savior armor and helmet as the central symbol in the narrative of the Saite dynasty and in its alliance with the Aegean world, and it's ironic opposed parallels in the narrative of the Davidic dynasty.

F. Saite-Aegean myths in a distorted mirror

F.1. The armor and helmet that saved the nation and its king

In its struggle with the Saites and their mercenaries, the Bible turns another weapon against them which it had pillaged from them: Egyptian-Aegean myths that were famous in that period. It seems that the words of Jeremiah were directed not only at the reality of the Aegean-Saite hoplites, but also against their ethos, which finds expression in a myth that originates in the reign of Psammeticus I. It is highly probable that the myth was also known in Judah, perhaps even during his reign through the mercenaries that Judah sent to him. The myth was certainly disseminated among the Judaeans when the pro-Egyptian party was dominant as propaganda means to gain support during the revolt against Babylon, and especially after the destruction of the Temple when many Jews fled to Egypt and settled there under Saite protection near the mercenaries.

The myth has a historical core: the rise to power of the Saite dynasty with the help of the Aegean hoplites; but it is wrapped within propagandist stories of miracles and wonders. The main role in the myth was played by their military equipment: the armor and helmets. Herodotus, who visited Egypt two hundred years later, between 459 to 454 BCE, tells the story. He admits that the history of Egypt before the Saites is less known to him, but 'ever since the Ionians and Carians have settled in Egypt… we Greeks through our intercourse with them have exact knowledge of the history of Egypt from the reign of Psammeticus and onwards' (II.154). After the conquest of Esarhaddon, Egypt had been divided into twelve provinces. Their governors formed an alliance, but waited for the realization of the oracle that the one who poured a wine offering from a bronze goblet to Hephaestus [identified with the Egyptian Ptah, S.R.] would rule all Egypt. It happened that Psammeticus did not have a goblet and he took off his bronze helmet and held it out and poured the libation with it. The other governors were afraid of him and exiled him to the marsh area. Then Psammeticus received the oracle that men with bronze armor and weapons would appear from the sea and come to his aid. And so it happened that Ionians and Carians who had gone out to the sea for piracy were forced to come ashore at that place. An Egyptian informed Psammeticus that bronze-clad people were plundering the coastal plain, since they had never before seen people armed with bronze weapons [the impression of the bronze-clad Greeks on the Egyptians was like that of the bronze-clad Goliath on the Israelites, S.R.]. But Psammeticus understood that these were his saviors. He made an alliance with them and with their help he conquered Egypt (II.151-152). He gave them lands for habitation on opposite sides of the arm of the Nile called the Pelusion, near the sea, a little way below the town of Bubastis. These places were called 'stratopeda' (military camps). Long afterwards, king Amasis removed them and settled them at Memphis to be his guard against the Egyptians. Herodotus saw their previous habitations and the remains of their homes and anchorage (II.154). The inscription of Ashurbanipal (A Prism) of 643/2 BCE confirms the historical core in the myth. It relates that Gugu, king of Ludu (Gyges Γύγης, the tyrant of Lydia Λυδία) sent Psammeticus some mercenaries after an agreement was made between them. Ashurbanipal castigates the treacherous Gyges who had asked him for help against the invasion of the Cimmerians but afterwards helped Egypt to revolt against him (Tadmor & Cogan 1977: 79).

The Saites also conducted an opportunistic and underhand foreign policy. At first they allied with Lydia against Assyria, and then with Assyria against Babylon. Necho II, Psammeticus II, Apries and Ahmose/Amasis II (570-526 BCE) continued to depend on a military and political alliance with the Aegean world (Herodotus III.40-43). Apries even used his mercenaries against his own people. This seems to be the reason for the empathy that Jeremiah demonstrates towards the suppressed Egyptians. Amasis was an army general who conducted a revolt against Apries and his mercenaries. When he came to power he also used them as his bodyguards and to protect his regime. He took them out of their camps and settled them near his palace in Memphis. It was only after the conquest of Egypt by Cambyses, king of Persia in 525 BCE that the mercenaries cease to be a dominant power in Egypt (Figs. 16-18).

The myth of the bronze-clad warriors served the interests of both sides. In addition to the divine legitimacy that it gave to Saite rule, it granted prestige to the rulers of Lydia and Greek soldiers. The Lydians at that time controlled Caria and a part of Ionia where they recruited the soldiers as mercenaries for the powers that fought each other. It was in Lydia that the first coins in the ancient world were minted. They also served as payment for the mercenaries and were quickly dispersed wherever they arrived.

The political and military partnership between the Saites and the Aegean world also included spiritual and religious affiliations in which the military equipment of the hoplites was given a supremely mystical significance. It constituted the symbol and legitimacy for the Saite regime which had succeeded through its help to liberate and unify Egypt and to establish an empire. Another story on the role played by the Aegean helmet in the rise to power of Psammeticus can be found in Polyaenus: 'He deposed Tementhes Τεμένθης king of Egypt in this way: Tementhes consulted the oracle of Amun about his kingdom and he was told to be careful of cocks. Πίγρες Pigres the Carian, who was an intimate friend of Psammeticus told him that the Carians were the first to use the crest feathers of cocks on their helmets. Psammeticus then understood the meaning of the oracle and recruited a large number of Carians into his service, and marched with them towards Memphis. He overthrew Tementhes in a battle near the Temple of Isis at a distance of 5 stades from the palace. This quarter in Memphis is now [in Herodotus' time, S.R.] called καρομεμφίται in name of these Carians' (Herodotus VII.3). Excavations in Memphis have exposed a stele of Pigres, which is identified by some scholars with the hero of the story (Williams & Villing 2006: 48).

Herodotus himself, a native of Halicarnasus the capital of Caria, whose father was a Carian, tells about the armor equipment that the Carians used. They invented the feather crest for the helmets, and were the first to put symbols on their shield, as well as the first to install handles for them. Until then the shields were carried only by a leather strap hung around the neck and over the left shoulder (I.171). The helmet was the emblem of royalty even when Amasis came to the throne: 'One of his soldiers put a helmet on his head and said he did so to crown him as king' (Herodotus II.162).

FIG. 16. AEGEAN HOPLITE ON AN IONIAN AMPHORA FROM DAPHNAE.
POTTERY: BLACK FIGURE NECK AMPHORA. DATE: 530 BCE (CIRCA). MADE IN: CLAZOMENAE (?),
IONIA, ASIA MINOR (TURKEY). ATTRIBUTED TO THE PETRIE PAINTER. FINDSPOT: TELL DAPHNAE,
"QASR", EAST ANNEX (G), CHAMBER 29, EGYPT. THE BRITISH MUSEUM, NO. 1888,0208.112.A
© THE TRUSTEES OF THE BRITISH MUSEUM.
TWO FRAGMENTS, RESTORED TOGETHER, OF UPPER BODY OF CLAZOMENIAN BLACK-FIGURED
SLIM NECK-AMPHORA: ARCHER, TWO HOPLITES FIGHTING.

Fig. 17. Aegean hoplite engraved on a relief from Naukratis.
Unfinished relief, probably once part of an architectural frieze. Date: 522-500 BCE (circa). Made in: Naukratis (?), Egypt. Findspot: Naukratis, Shrine of Aphrodite (Panhellenion-Temenos), Egypt. The British Museum, No. 1900,0214.21.© The Trustees of the British Museum.
Armed man walking to right, with crested Corinthian helmet, spear and shield held out in front, the inner side being shown. The rear leg has the heel raised and shows the scratched outline of a greave.

Fig. 18. Carian skyphos from Naukrtis.
Date: 7th century BCE. Made in: Caria. Findspot: Naukratis, Egypt. The British Museum, No. 1888,0601.653. © The Trustees of the British Museum.
Sherd from body of pottery skyphos; black glaze inside; fields on the outside divided by vertical and horizontal lines; bird.

Hoplite armor also became the symbol of Saite-Aegean victory and conquest of the Land of Israel. Herodotus relates that Pharaoh Necho 'with his foot soldiers [hoplites] encountered Syrians near Migdol [the reference is to Josiah in Megiddo in 609 BCE, S.R.] and was victorious over them, and after his victory he conquered the large Syrian city of Kaditis [the reference is to the conquest of Gaza in 601 BCE after he had repulsed Nebuchadnezzar's attempt to invade Egypt. S.R.] He sent the armor in which he carried out these victories to the Branchidai temple in Miletus and dedicated it to Apollo' (Herodotus II.159). [Herodotus calls the oracle of Apollo in Dydima 'Branchidai' (Branchidians) according to the name of the priestly dynasty that conducted it. S. R.]. Amasis repeated the act of Necho in dedicating his armor to the Temple of Athena in Lindos in Rhodes (ibid. III.47). From the fact that the battle-armors were not dedicated to Egyptian gods but to the gods of the mercenaries, it is clear that it was to them that the Saites ascribed their victories. The dedications were doubtless published not only in Egypt and the Aegean world, but in Judah as well where it symbolized its humiliation and the end of its national freedom. Moreover, they symbolized the double defeat of the God of Israel by the gods of Egypt and Greece, both in the international arena, since the Deut. cycles supported the expansionist policy of Josiah, and internally, since the worship of idols recommenced with the ascension of Jehoiakim to the throne.

The dedications are understandable in view of the strong ties between Egyptian and Greek theology. The Egyptians and the Greeks developed a system of identification between their gods. Athena, goddess of war, wisdom and weaving and the patron of Athens and Lindos, was identified with Neith, the main goddess of Lower Egypt (Herodotus II.28). Neith was a goddess of war and carried a shield with two crossed arrows. She reached the height of her power in the Saite period. They were proud of their victories and restored ancient cultic rites, and installed their tombs in the walls of her temple. Neith created the serpent of darkness Apep (Apophis) and Athena created the monster Medusa, and engraved on her shield the shape of its head adorned with serpent tresses. These two goddesses were the patrons of crafts and weaving. Neith was the creation goddess who attached the heavens to her loom, wove the world, and then created all the animals. She is also the cow of the heavens, and also the cow that swam in the sea and rose to the shores of the Delta to indicate the place where Sais would be erected. Neith was identified with Hathor, with Isis, and with the Canaanite Ashtoreth and Anath (on the archaeological findings of the temples in the cities of the Delta, and the cults and temple building during the 25th and 26th dynasties, see: P. Wilson 2010; C. Zivie-Coche 2008).

The magnificent armor that the Saites contributed aroused amazement among the Greeks. They were so greatly desired that Sparta went to war against Samos because its men had stolen the armor that Amasis had sent it as a gift. The armor was made of linen embroidered with gold and many pictorial designs. It was also woven with cotton threads, and each thread, in spite of being fine-spun, comprised 360 visible filaments (Herodotus III.47). A similar armor was sent by Amasis to the Temple of Athena in Lindos, together with two stone statues of himself. This was because the construction of the temple was attributed to the daughters of Danaus who came from Egypt. The full name of Amasis was 'Chenibra Amose son of Neith'. It is no wonder that he dedicated to his Greek 'mother' this wondrous creation of warfare and weaving. Because of his friendship with Polycrates he also contributed to the

Temple of Hera in Samos, but there he only dedicated two statues of himself made of wood. Amasis made a substantial contribution to renovate the Temple of Apollo in Delphi after it was burned (ibid. II.182). During his long reign the close ties between Egypt and Greece reached its zenith. He married Ladike Λαδικη, a Grecian woman from Cyrene whom he loved more than all his wives (ibid. II.178). In contrast with their openness to the Greeks, the Saites turned their backs to the East. They fought against Assyria, Babylon and Persia. According to Herodotus, the refusal of Amasis to give his daughter in marriage to Cambyses the son of Cyrus was the cause for the conquest of Egypt by the Persians (ibid. III.1).

Another reason for the dedication of the armor is suggested by Murray. He claims that the temples, especially in Delphi and Branchidai, were turned into mercenary recruiting centers for the rulers of Lydia and Egypt. Pilgrims and participants in festivals looked at their magnificent gifts to the temple and were persuaded by the wealth of the employers. Amasis allowed Greek merchants to settle in Naukratis. An international trade circle was created in which Egypt exported grain and received in exchange silver metal with which it paid the mercenaries, and these spent their money again in the Aegean world. Thus, this dynasty that had conducted return to sources in religion and art, was forced to disrupt the economy of Egypt in order to maintain massive foreign forces within it (2001: 235).

In contrast with the Aegean-Saite myth, the Bible sets up an opposing myth, on the elaborate armor that failed and the helmet that did not save the Philistine/Aegean warrior who cursed the God of Israel. He is defeated by a lad 'naked' of armor and weapons who fought God's war. Goliath represents the army of Necho and David the army of Josiah. This explains the ideological and literary affinities between the prophecies of Jeremiah on the Saites and their mercenaries and the story of David and Goliath.

F.2. Deliverance of the army by a hero in a duel with an armed giant

In those days, at the turn of the 7th century BCE, another widespread myth was associated with the duel with an Aegean warrior, this time a mercenary in the service of Babylon. It was told in a poem composed by Alcaeus to celebrate the return of his brother, the hero Antimenidas, from ends of the earth. Strabo quotes a part of it in prose:

'ἔσχεν ἐνδόξους τὸ παλαιὸν μὲν Πιττακόν, ἕνα τῶν ἑπτὰ σοφῶν, καὶ τὸν ποιητὴν Ἀλκαῖον καὶ τὸν ἀδελφὸν Ἀντιμενίδαν, ὅν φησιν Ἀλκαῖος Βαβυλωνίοις συμμαχοῦντα τελέσαι μέγαν ἆθλον καὶ ἐκ πόνων αὐτοὺς ῥύσασθαι κτείναντα 'ἄνδρα μαχαίταν βασιληίων παλαστὰν (ὥς φησιν) ἀπολείποντα μόνον μίαν παχέων ἀπὺ πέμπων' (13.2.3). (Mitylene has produced famous men in early times such as Pittacus, one of the Seven Wise Men; and the poet Alcaeus, and his brother Antimenidas, who, according to Alcaeus, 'won a great struggle when fighting on the side of the Babylonians, and rescued them from their toils by killing a warrior (as he says), who was but one palm short of five royal cubits in height' [about 216 cm, S.R.].

The first two lines of the poem, which we received through Hephaestion of Alexandria, *Handbook on Metres* (*Enciridion* x.3) and Libanius of Antioch (*Oratio* 13.5) (apud: Campbell 385-386), tells that Antimenidas brought as booty a sword made of gold and ivory:

'ἦλθες ἐκ περάτων γᾶς, ἐλεφαντίναν / λάβαν τῶ ξίφεος χρυσοδέταν / ἔχων'.

Some scholars believe that Antimenidas participated in the campaign of Nebuchadnezzar in 604 BCE, because elsewhere Alcaeus tells about a war of 'holy Babylon' and Ashqelon (Frg. 131/48), but the name of Antimenidas is missing from this fragment. Perhaps it refers to the campaign of 601 BCE against Egypt. A Babylonian chronicle (BM 33041) relates that Nebuchadnezzar conducted another campaign in the 37th year of his reign (i.e. 567 BCE) when he went to Egypt to fight against Amasis who recruited his friends or allies from the city of Putu-Iaman, from distant regions in the islands in the midst of the sea (*ANET*, Pritchard 1950: 308, c. II). The document is cut short and the end is missing. 'Iamani' in Assyrian and Babylonian documents means 'Greek'. Winckler interprets the name 'Putu' as Pittacus (1897: 511). For others, 'Putu' is Put, i.e. Libya. According to Wiseman, the meaning of the term is archers, and the reference is to the Greek mercenaries whom Nebuchadnezzar had captured and brought to Babylon (1956: 94-95). He also believes that the campaign was conducted during the final days of Apries, when he shared the throne with Amasis (idem 1991: 39-40). The chronicle conforms with the prophecy of Jeremiah (43: 8-13) that Nebuchadnezzar would conquer Egypt, but perhaps it had as background only the information about the projected campaign (Hoffman 2001: 734-735). We do not have any further sources on this matter. Josephus does mention the invasion of Egypt by Nebuchadnezzar in the fifth year after the destruction of Jerusalem, his execution of the king and the crowning of another in his place, and that he took the Jews of Egypt to Babylon (*Antiquities*, X, 182-183), but it seems he based this on Jeremiah.

Alcaeus and Antimenidas were the rivals of Pittacus. At first the tyrants of the Penthilus family ruled until the last of them was murdered. The brothers of Alcaeus cooperated with Pittacus to eliminate the next tyrant, Melanchrus, who ruled under the protection of Lydia, but later on Pittacus assisted the new tyrant Myrsilus and became an enemy of Alcaeus' family. Then war broke out over Sigeion during which Alcaeus cast aside his shield while Pittacus defeated Phrynon. With the death of Myrsilus, Pittacus married into the Penthilid family and thus paved his way to the throne. He exiled his rivals or sent them far away to fight as mercenaries. Alcaeus and Antimenidas despaired of returning to Lesbos and went wandering in foreign lands. According to Strabo, Alcaeus visited Egypt (1.2.30). If Amasis had ties with Pittacus who, according to Plutarch, received from him a severed tongue in answer to his question which organ was the best and the worst in the body (*Moralia* frg. 89 Sandbach; cf. *Moralia* 506C *De garrulitate*), then the preference of Antimenidas to serve in the army of Nebuchadnezzar, the enemy of Amasis, is understandable. When Pittacus realized that his country could not be maintained without a warrior caste, he brought back the exiled. He said that mercy is better than vengeance (Diogenes Laetius I.76). In this he also resembles David who was wont to forgive his enemies. Alcaeus apparently found his death as a mercenary of Lydia in the battle against the Allienoi (*Papyrus Oxyrhynchus* 2506 Treu M. 1966 in: Kaplan 2002: 234). Antimenidas, like David, was venerated as a hero over many generations. Strabo lists him among the famous personalities in Mytilene, on the same level as Pittacus and Alcaeus.

Also the Greeks had a negative view of γίγαντες which symbolized aggressive power play, hubris, arrogance, and the violation of cosmic order. In the theogony it is told that they rebelled against the Olympic gods, were defeated in battle (the 'Gigantomachia') and were thrown into Tartarus. Hesiod describes their metal armor equipment as similar to that of the hoplites:

'...τε Γίγαντας

τεύχεσι λαμπομένους, δολίχ' ἔγχεα χερσὶν ἔχοντας'

(Giants with gleaming armour, holding long spears in their hands) (*Theogony* 185-186).

The Gigantomachia became a popular subject from the beginning of the 7th century BCE. It was portrayed on black-figured vases, in the northern frieze reliefs of the Siphnian Treasury in Delphi, in the pediment of the old Temple of Athena on the Acropolis in Athens, and in metopes on the eastern frieze of the Parthenon (*LIMC* IV, 1988; Moore 1995: 633-639). In every period it received some allegorical significance related to that time, such as the struggle between the Greeks and the Persians after the Persian wars, or between Alexander the Great and the peoples of the East (Mayerson 2001: 68). The giants in Delphi, and also the black-figured ones on vases are always portrayed as hoplites with heavy military equipment, a short chiton and armor, greaves, Corinthian helmets with a high or low crest, armed with shields, spear and sword, and sometimes with stones. Among the gods that fought against them, only Ares is portrayed as a hoplite. Later on, on red-figured vases – perhaps under the influence of their description in the pediment of the new Temple of Athena on the Acropolis – the giants are naked, but are still armed with helmet, shield, and spear or sword (Brandt 1988: 10-40, 95-96, 184-186, 219-221).

G. The story of the duel in light of the biblical attitude to the Babylonian exiles and the Egyptian diaspora

The biblical editor was not unaware of the similarities that could be drawn between the arrival of the Saite mercenaries to Egypt and Canaan, and the arrival of the Sea Peoples, including the Philistines, to Egypt centuries earlier. They were also from the Aegean world, and they as well were experienced warriors who came to Egypt for purposes of intrusion and plunder. They, too, were recruited into the service of the Pharaohs and became their loyal mercenaries and protectors of their regime. At first they were housed in fortresses or army camps, and later were settled and did not return to their homeland. The story of the duel, which had an ancient core, was given prominence during the days when Josiah confronted the Saite-Greek world. The Philistines were still the territorial and religious enemy until in the final decade of the 7th century BCE Nebuchadnezzar conquered their cities, destroyed them and exiled the people to Babylon. The message of this story – that there is no value in the superior excellence of the hoplite and Aegean armor – remained valid even after that, when the Saites incited Judah to rebel against Babylon and promised her military aid. But a philological and literary analysis of the story shows that its compilation and editing continued after the destruction, and also during Second Temple times. This means that the importance of this message did not lessen, even when the confrontation with the Philistines or Saites was no longer relevant. The question is: Why and in what circumstances was the interest in it prolonged?

After the destruction of the First Temple, the story of the duel had no significance for the devastated land of Judah, nor among the Jews in Babylonian exile. From Babylonian documents it appears that the number of Greeks in Mesopotamia during the 6th and 5th centuries BCE was minimal and their status was not high. There were some Cilicians that the Babylonians employed as carpenters, perhaps in building ships, as well as Ionians. Some Carians were there, apparently as mercenaries captured from Egypt during the military campaign of Nebuchadnezzar against it and who were exiled to Babylon. They lived in settlements as the tenants of the king. Carian captives were also exiled to Babylon by Cambyses, king of Persia, who conquered Egypt in 525 BCE (Zadok 2005: 79-82). Therefore, it seems to me that Egypt was the only place in which the message of the story was relevant and of highest importance, since the motivation of the story was the great fear of Egyptian-Greek influence on the Jewish diaspora that was being formed there in those days. This diaspora consisted of migrant Jews who had already arrived there before the destruction, and the 'remnant of Judah' that fled there after Gedaliah the son of Ahikam, the governor appointed by the Babylonians, was murdered by Ishmael the son of Nethaniah. The attitude of the Bible towards this diaspora was extremely negative. It is especially noticeable in Jeremiah, who was taken by force to Egypt by the leaders of those who fled. His attitude is in polar opposition to the one he shows towards the Jews in Babylonian exile. The first among those exiled with Jehoiachin were called 'good figs' in contrast to the 'bad figs' that remained in Judah under the rule of Zedekiah (Jeremiah

24: 1-2). They are the 'holy seed' of the people with whom God keeps his everlasting covenant. While Jeremiah and Ezekiel promised the exiles redemption and restoration, those remaining in Judah and those who had migrated to Egypt were destined to be cut off and destroyed.[24] The reason for this profound bias were the differences between the two diasporas which were most marked at their beginning.

The first basic difference lay in the circumstances in which they were formed. While Jews in Babylon were compelled to go there, those who migrated to Egypt did so by choice. According to Oded, the term גָּלוּת 'galut' (exile) had the negative connotation of being uprooted, expelled, enforced change of place. The term פְּזוּרָה 'pezura' (diaspora) has the neutral meaning of migration and settlement by free will outside the homeland with the permanent option of returning to it. From the viewpoint of possibility or ideology, exile has an ending while the diaspora, which was formed by choice, represents 'endless exile' (2008: 85). In this lies the second essential difference, in their moral and religious character; and therefore, according to the Bible, also their chances for redemption. The fact is that those exiled to Babylon recognized their guilt. They internalized the view of the prophets that the exile was a punishment for their sins and the sins of their fathers. Their remorse and yearnings for Zion were the cause for their moral and religious reformation. In the absence of a temple as the center of religious life and cultic ritual, the ritual of prayer was developed amongst them. Smith-Christopher stresses the theological importance of prayers, remorse and supplications. The shame for the sins of their fathers led to the possibility of change and promise that they would no longer sin (2002: 122-123). According to Rofé, Jeremiah placed the idea of repentance above all else (Jeremiah 2: 33-35; 3: 1-5; 12: 2-13; 19: 20): 'He rejected the easy and lighthearted repentance that is sure of forgiveness. He sought for the consciousness of sin and the pangs of conscience, and what emerges from it: tears and despair (Jeremiah 3: 21; 4: 1). These alone would cleanse the sinners from their wrongdoing, until God returns and brings them back to him' (Rofé 1986: 107). Jeremiah promises that God would forgive those in Babylon and would limit their exile to seventy years. When they returned they would crown a descendant of the House of David to rule over them (Jeremiah 24: 7; 29: 6-10).

Ezekiel rebukes the exiles in Babylon for their adherence to the idolatry they had brought with them from Canaan, and for the activities of the false prophets and magicians among them (Ezekiel 13: 1-9, 17-23). But they heeded his admonishments and he was regarded by them as their moral guide. 'The elders of the community' used to come to his home and sit listening to the words of God without remonstrance. Ezekiel also prophesied redemption for them, but the reasons were different. The return to Zion was promised in spite of their sins and with no connection to their remorse. The reason for it was the desire of God to keep them unique and separate from the idol-worshipping nations, even against their will, so that He alone would rule over them: 'And that which cometh into

---

[24] In both books, Jeremiah and Ezekiel, the version of the MT differs from the Septuagint. One approach is to regard the Septuagint as reflecting an earlier version, since the MT is longer and includes additions that are sometimes in the form of detailed explanations and interpretations of the original version. (Tov 1990, 'Ezekiel': 17; 'Jeremiah': 19). According to another approach, the MT is the original and the Septuagint includes later editing of the Prophets that were not introduced into the manuscript of the MT. The books were compiled at the beginning of the Second Temple period under Persian rule, and comprised emendations, additions and interpretations by the disciples of the prophets (Rofé 2007: 257-258, 285-286).

your mind shall not be at all, that ye say, We will be as the heathen, as the families of the countries, to serve wood and stone. …with a stretched out arm, and with fury poured out, will I rule over you' (ibid. 20: 32-33). They will be taken out of Babylon with a 'strong arm' just as in the exodus from Egypt, in order to show the nations the power of God. Just as then, he would bring the people into the desert and judge them there. Only the chosen would return to Zion, while the sinners would not even return to their place of exile. The worship of God would be renewed in Jerusalem, and the return to Zion would lead to the recognition of God's greatness by the returning exiles and by the entire world: '…when I shall bring you out from the people, and gather you out of the countries where in ye have been scattered; and I will be sanctified in you before the heathen. And ye shall know that I am the Lord, when I shall bring you into the land of Israel, into the country for the which I lifted up mine hand to give it to your fathers' (ibid. 20: 41-42). Only then will the returning exiles recognize their sins and be filled with shame and mortification: '…and ye shall loathe yourselves in your own sight for all your evils that ye have committed. And ye shall know that I am the Lord, when I have wrought with you for my name's sake' (ibid. 43-44). Then the rule of the House of David will be renewed as well: 'And I will set up one shepherd over them, and he shall feed them, even my servant David … And I the Lord will be their God, and my servant David a prince among them' (ibid. 34: 23-24). The redemption of the people will be carried out by force and violence while shame, remorse and the knowledge of God are not the reasons for it but its result.

The prophets apparently did not fear that the exiles would adopt the religion of Babylon and become assimilated within it. The Second Isaiah, Jeremiah and Habbakuk described the expected downfall of Babylon with which its gods, Bel, Nebo and Marduk would also collapse. But there is no public battle between them and God. Ezekiel does not attack the religion of Babylon and does not prophesy destruction for its gods, and there is only an implicit irony in his description of Nebuchadnezzar who 'consulted with images, he looked in the liver' in order to decide whether to destroy Ammon first or Judah (Ezekiel 21: 26). Ornan even claims that there is some ideological affinity between the Babylonian and Judaic religion. On one hand there was a religious trend in Mesopotamia that was opposed to the iconization of the gods. Their images were not displayed in public but were kept enclosed in temples into which only the priests could enter. On the other hand, even God was described in a human image as derived from the verse: 'Let us make man in our image, after our likeness' (Genesis 1: 26-27). Isaiah describes God in the form of a man sitting in the Temple in Jerusalem (Isaiah 6: 1). The prohibition was only in worshiping the image. Therefore, in her opinion, the Bible was not opposed to the religion of Babylon (Ornan 2005: 109-182).

But the main reason that there was no danger for the assimilation of the exiles in a foreign land was their loyalty to Zion and Jerusalem as their sole and eternal homeland, the center and very purpose for their existence: 'How shall we sing the Lord's song in a strange land. If I forget thee, O Jerusalem, let my right hand forget her cunning. If I do not remember thee, let my tongue cleave to the roof of my mouth; if I prefer not Jerusalem above my chief joy' (Psalms 137: 4-6). They are not even interested in erecting a temple as a cultic center that would rival the one in Jerusalem. Their spiritual conduct focused on preserving and practicing the law of Moses. Even if many of the Jews in Babylon did not return and preferred to wait for messianic times, their religious affiliation with Zion guarded them against assimilation.

The preservation of the social and cultural frameworks they had brought with them from their homeland also protected their spiritual immunity. The Jews were settled in Babylon in accordance with their original communities. The Babylonians did the same with the other inhabitants of cities and countries they had conquered and exiled (Eph'al 1978: 80-83; Zadok 1978: 57-65; Oded 2000: 91-104). From Babylonian records it seems that Jehoiachin retained his title 'King of Judah' (*ANET*, Pritchard 1950: 308, c. I). The leaders of the exiles were 'Elders of the Exile' (in Judah they were called 'Elders of the Community'). As in Judah, the spiritual leadership included priests, levites and prophets. Thanks to this, they could lead the people in the Return to Zion and the building of the Second Temple with Zerubbabel the grandson of Jehoiachin, Joshua (named in Zechariah 3: 2 as 'a brand plucked out of the fire', because he had survived the destruction) the grandson of Seraiah the last high priest, and Ezra the scribe, son of Seraiah.

The Book of Kings ends with the story of the release of Jehoiachin from prison by Evil-Merodach, king of Babylon, while the Book of Chronicles ends with the declaration of Cyrus: 'Now in the first year of Cyrus king of Persia, that the word of the Lord spoken by the mouth of Jeremiah might be accomplished, the Lord stirred up the spirit of Cyrus king of Persia, that he made a proclamation throughout all his kingdom, and put it also into writing, saying. Thus saith Cyrus king of Persia, All the kingdoms of the earth hath the Lord God of heaven given me; and he hath charged me to build him a house in Jerusalem, which is in Judah. Who is there among you of all his people? The Lord his God be with him, and let him go up' (II Chronicles 36: 22-23).

The end is an optimistic one: the hope for the revival of the people in its land, thanks to world recognition of the greatness of God. This is the answer to Heard who rejects the presentation of Deut. history as a national epic (in which the story of David and Goliath is a part) because of its tragic end in destruction and exile. In fact, it was the exile itself that had created the opportunity for remorse, repentance, moral reform, and perfect adherence to Mosaic law, while the reforms that the kings and prophets tried to carry out during the period of the Kingdom of Judah did not have any deep effect upon the people. The exiles in Babylon were granted redemption and Zerubbabel, the grandson of Jehoiachin, who was appointed the governor of Judah, led those who returned to Zion in building the Second Temple.

But a large part of the Jewish people – the 'remnants of Judah' as well as those who had migrated to Egypt before the destruction – did not undergo the process of purification, repentance and atonement, and therefore it was faced with the danger of annihilation. As in the days of the Kingdom of Judah, the source of danger was not Babylon but Saite Egypt.

Jeremiah witnessed the realization of his prophecies on the destruction of the kingdom and Temple and the exile to Babylon. But the greatest national and personal catastrophe still lay before him. The continued settlement and cultivation of the land by the 'remnants of Judah' was in his eyes a divine command. He himself redeemed a field from his cousin a year before the destruction while he was in prison as a sign that 'Houses and fields and vineyards shall be possessed again in this land' (Jeremiah 32: 15). In his prophecies the negative aspects of the city, the royal court and the Temple are stressed: Jehoiakim 'buildeth his house by unrighteousness, and his chambers by wrong' (ibid. 22:13). He mocks those who regard the Temple as a guarantee for the immunity of Jerusalem and Judah. Jeremiah warns of destruction and exile, but hoped that if it came, the wild weeds in society would be uprooted. He had confidence in the forces of growth and infinite renewal of nature, and saw in the cultivation of the land the chance for national revival and moral and social reform. With this would come redemption and from the House of David a king, a 'righteous branch', would flourish and his name would be 'the Lord our righteousness' (ibid. 23: 5-6; 33: 15-16). Indeed, the hope for revival sprouted immediately after the destruction. Nebuchadnezzar appointed Gedaliah the son of Ahikam as governor over the 'remnant of Judah'. Jeremiah was given the choice of going wherever he wished, and he joined Gedaliah in Mizpah. It was not necessary for him to go to Babylon with the exiles; Ezekiel was there to guide them, and there the descendant of the House of David would flower. He wanted to remain in Judah where he redeemed his family inheritance as a symbol for the continued commitment of the people to the land. 'Likewise when all the Jews that were in Moab, and among the Ammonites, and in Edom, and that were in all the countries, heard that the king of Babylon had left a remnant of Judah ... Even all the Jews returned out of all the places whither they were driven, and came to the land of Judah, to Gedaliah, unto Mizpah, and gathered wine and summer fruits very much' (ibid. 40: 11-12).

But the hope was cut off in its prime. Ishmael the son of Nethaniah conspired with Baalis, king of Ammon and murdered Gedaliah and the Babylonian guard forces, took all the rest of the people as captives and led them towards Ammon. The heads of the army led by Johanan the son of Kareah thwarted his plans and released the people, but for fear of revenge by Babylon, they set out for Egypt. On the way they asked Jeremiah to seek the word of God: 'Let, we beseech thee, our supplication be accepted before thee, and pray for us unto the Lord thy God, even for all this remnant ... The Lord be a true and faithful witness between us, if we do not even according to all things for the which the Lord thy God shall send thee to us. And he said to them ... If ye will still abide in this land, then will I build you, and not pull you down, and I will plant you, and not pluck you up; for I repent me of the evil I have done unto you. Be not afraid of the king of Babylon ... for I am with you to save you, and to deliver you from his hand. And I will shew mercies unto you, that he may have mercy upon you, and cause you to return to your own land. But if ye say, We will not dwell in this land ... but we will go to the land of Egypt ... As mine anger and my fury hath been poured forth upon the inhabitants of Jerusalem; so shall my fury be poured forth upon you, when ye shall enter into Egypt; and ye shall be an execration, and an astonishment, and a curse, and a reproach, and ye shall see this place no more. The Lord hath said concerning you, O ye remnant of Judah: Go ye not into Egypt' (ibid. 42: 1-19).

Like many kings in the Ancient East, the kings of Israel and Judah sometimes sought the word of God through the prophets, but if this did not suit their policy, they might not listen to it (Hoffman 1994: 85-88). Thus Saul and Samuel in Michmash, Ahab and Michaihu the son of Imlah, Zedekiah and Jeremiah. According to the Bible, the result of their refusal to listen was always destructive. Also the army captains and the remnants of Judah did not accept the decree of God. They made a law for themselves, and thus emptied the concepts of good and evil, sin and punishment, redemption and forgiveness, of all their contents. Their alienation is reflected in the phrase 'the Lord thy God'. When Jeremiah exposes their denial the 'wicked men' accuse him of lies and treason saying that God did not forbid them to go down to Egypt, and he was incited by Baruch the son of Neriah to deliver them to the Babylonians (Jeremiah 43: 2-6). They took Jeremiah and Baruch: '[and] came into the land of Egypt; for they obeyed not the voice of the Lord; thus came they even to Tahpanhes' (ibid. 43: 7).

Why did Jeremiah adamantly object to the descent into Egypt? Here is where the analogy between him and Moses should be stressed. It is accepted in research that the Book of Deuteronomy is the 'book of the law of the Lord given by Moses' or the 'book of the covenant' that was found in the Temple during the reign of Josiah (II Chronicles 34: 14) and inspired his religious reform. It said there that Moses forbade the people to return to Egypt: 'But he shall not ... cause the people to return to Egypt ... and the Lord hath said unto you, Ye shall henceforth return no more that way' (Deuteronomy 17: 16). Chapter 11 in Jeremiah is an exhortation to keep the covenant. The prophet regarded the freedom from slavery and the exodus from Egypt as the formative event in the history of Israel (Hoffman 1990: 127-128). In his own time he regarded the descent to Egypt as worse than death, and that all who went there would never return. Jehoahaz who was exiled there was more miserable than the dead Josiah: 'Weep ye not for the dead, neither bemoan him; but weep sore for him that goeth away; for he shall return no more, nor see his native country ... But he shall die in the place whither they have led him captive, and shall see this land no more' (Jeremiah 22: 10-12). Therefore, the remnant of Judah who have given up their independence and homeland are worse than the generation of the desert that wanted to return to the 'house of slavery' because the latter had never experienced a life of independence in its homeland.

Moreover, the settlement of the Israelites in the promised land was the proof of their being the chosen people and of maintaining the covenant between Abraham and God. Moses sent spies to tour the country, but they returned in fright after forty days and reported: 'We will not be able to go up against the people; for they are stronger than we. And they brought up an evil report of the land which they had searched ... saying, The land through which we have gone to search it, is a land that eateth up the inhabitants thereof; and all the people that we saw were of a great stature. And there we saw the giants, the sons of Anak, which come of the giants; and we were in our own sight as grasshoppers, and so were we in their sight' (Numbers 13: 31-33). This parallels the forty days of dread in confronting Goliath, the internalizing of enemy propaganda and adoption of a negative self-image. The desert generation rebelled against God: 'And wherefore hat the Lord brought us unto this land, to fall by the sword, that our wives and our children should be a prey ... And they said to one another, Let us make a captain, and let us return into Egypt. And Moses and Aaron fell on their faces .... And said ... If the Lord delight in us, then he will bring us into this land and give it us... Only rebel not ye against the Lord, neither fear ye the people of the land ... and the Lord is with us ...But all the congregation bade stone them with stones' (Numbers 14: 2-10). Their punishment was to die in the desert, and Moses their leader with them. Jeremiah, like Moses, was perceived by the people as expressing the word of God. He was also met with rejection, persecution and attempted murder. The similarities between Moses and Jeremiah is already inherent in their inauguration into prophecy: 'And Moses said unto the Lord, O my Lord, I am not eloquent, neither heretofore, nor since thou hast spoken to thy servant; but I am slow of speech, and of a slow tongue ... And the Lord said unto him ... Now therefore go, and I will be with thy mouth, and teach thee what thou shalt say' (Exodus 4: 10-12). And Jeremiah says: 'Ah, Lord God! behold, I cannot speak: for I am a child. But the Lord said unto me, Say not, I am a child: for thou shalt go to all that I shall send thee, and whatsoever I command thee thou shalt speak ... Then the Lord put forth his hand, and touched my mouth, And the Lord said unto me, Behold, I have put my words in thy mouth' (Jeremiah 1: 6-9). Their fate is similar in their deaths outside the promised land, among the 'desert generation' that rejected the promised land. But the geographical, political and personal path of Jeremiah is opposite to the one of Moses. He is forced to participate in abandoning the homeland, in the breakup of the political framework and renunciation of freedom, and in accepting the status of refugees and protégées in a foreign country. His standing is not that of a leader but of a captive led by force.

The second difference led to the consolidation of monotheism among the Babylonian exiles, while the Jews in Egypt tended towards polytheism. The uniqueness of God was the first commandment and the basis of the Jewish faith. It is bound up with the liberation from Egypt, which was the source of the commitment of Israel to its God: 'I am the Lord thy God, which have brought thee out of the land of Egypt, out of the house of bondage. Thou shalt have no other gods before me' (Exodus 20: 2-3; Deuteronomy 5: 6-7). There was a severe prohibition against Egyptian idolatry (Leviticus 18: 2) and especially the cult of heavenly bodies that were designated to be the gods of other nations: 'And lest thou lift up thine eyes unto heaven, and when thou seest the sun, and the moon, and the stars, even all the host of heaven, shouldest be driven to worship them, and serve them, which the Lord thy God hath divided unto all the nations under the whole heaven. But the Lord hath taken you, and brought you forth out of the iron furnace, even out of Egypt, to be unto him a people of inheritance, as ye are this day' (Deuteronomy 4: 19-20). God himself goes out to battle with the gods of Egypt. In the exodus from Egypt: 'For I will pass through the land of Egypt this night, and will smite all the firstborn ... and against all the gods of Egypt I will execute judgment: I am the Lord...when I smite the land of Egypt' (Exodus 12: 12-13). According to Jeremiah, God will do this again when Nebuchadnezzar comes: 'And when he cometh, he will smite the land of Egypt... And I will kindle a fire in the houses of the gods of Egypt; and he shall burn them, and carry them away captives ... He shall break also the monuments of Beth shemesh that is in the land of Egypt; and the houses of the gods of the Egyptians shall he burn with fire' (Jeremiah 43: 11-13). It seems that these were obelisks that the Pharaohs dedicated to the sun cult in On-Heliopolis. Two of them were set up a short while before Jeremiah arrived in Egypt by Psammeticus II. As we saw above, according to Ezekiel as well, God himself will destroy the gods of Egypt.

Moses provided the basis for the unique faith and cult, but Jeremiah was witness to its disintegration. The migrants publicly worshipped the 'malkat ha'shamayim' (queen of heaven), which is the term for the Mesopotamian goddess Ishtar (Hoffman 2001: 744), and the biblical distortion of her name here - 'mlechet ha'shamayim' - was intentional (Ben Yosef Tawil 2009: 408). If the first Jews in Egypt were mercenaries sent by King Manasseh, it may be understood why they adhered to her. Manasseh was influenced by the religion of Assyria and built altars in the Temple courtyards to the 'hosts of heaven', in addition to renewing the cult of Baal and Asherah (II Kings 21). In Canaan the queen of heaven was identified with Ashtoreth, whose cult was widespread in Judah (Jeremiah 7: 18). Both of them were identified in Egypt with Isis and Neith, who were also goddesses of the heaven, fertility and war. In Chapter 44, Jeremiah pours out his anger: '… concerning all the Jews which dwell in the land of Egypt, which dwell in Migdol, and at Tahpanhes, and at Noph, and in the country of Pathros, saying … Wherefore commit ye this great evil against your souls … In that ye provoke me unto wrath with the works of your hands, burning incense unto other gods in the land of Egypt, whither ye be gone to dwell, that ye might cut yourselves off, and that ye might be a curse and a reproach among all the nations of the earth? … For I will punish them that dwell in the land of Egypt, as I have punished Jerusalem, by the sword, by the famine, and by the pestilence. So that none of the remnant of Judah, which are gone into the land of Egypt to sojourn there, shall escape or remain , that they should return into the land of Judah, to the which they have a desire to return to dwell there; for none shall return but such as shall escape'. But those listening to him removed their mask of piety which they had worn before, and rejected his rebukes altogether: 'Then all the men which knew that their wives had burned incense to other gods, and all the women that stood by, a great multitude, even all the people that dwelt in the land of Egypt, in Pathros, answered Jeremiah, saying. As for the word that thou has spoken unto us in the name of the Lord we will not hearken unto thee. But we will certainly do whatsoever thing goeth forth out of our own mouth, to burn incense unto the queen of heaven, and to pour out drink offerings unto her, as we have done, we, and our fathers, our kings, and our princes, in the cities of Judah, and in the streets of Jerusalem: for then we had plenty of victuals and were well, and saw no evil. But since we left off to burn incense to the queen of heaven, and to pour out drink offerings unto her, we have wanted all those things, and have been consumed by the sword and by the famine' (ibid. 44: 1-18). The despair of Jeremiah over the Jews of Egypt and his realization that they were beyond rectification, can be understood in the light of the historical and theological 'lesson' they had learnt: that the destruction and exile were actually the punishment for the reforms of Josiah. The Babylonian exiles had also committed the sin of idolatry, but they accepted the rebuke of Ezekiel and recognized their wrongdoing. Jeremiah himself prophesied for them, even before the destruction, forgiveness and the return to Zion, contrary to those remaining in Judah (Chapter 29).

The Jews from the land of Pathros were mercenaries and their families who lived in settlements in Yeb and Syene/Swene and protected the border with Nubia. Their polytheistic cult is known to us from hundreds of *papyri* and *ostraca* written in Aramaic of the 6th and 5th centuries BCE that were found there (Porten 1968). Their temple was built before the Persian conquest, during the Saite period. There they worshipped Yahu (Jehovah) and his consort Anath-Yahu (like the pair of 'Jehovah and his Asherah' in the inscriptions from Kuntillet 'Ajrud and Khirbet el-Qom). Anat, the warring maiden, the patroness of the the castes of warriors in Canaan and Phoenicia, was also adored in Egypt and identified with Neith. By erecting the temple, the mercenaries in Yeb (Elephantine) transgressed the prohibition to set up altars and high places outside the Temple in Jerusalem. Biblical historiography ascribed the destruction of the Kingdom of Samaria to the erection of an altar in Bethel and in the religious schism caused by Jeroboam the son of Nabat. The Babylonian exiles accepted the stance of Ezekiel that only in Jerusalem 'on my holy mount' would it be possible to rebuild the temple and renew the cult, as the necessary condition for the redemption of the people and also of its recognition, and the recognition of the entire world, in the greatness of God. The fear was that the erection of a temple in Egypt would weaken the spiritual need of the migrants to return to Judah. In the opinion of Porten, the temple in Yeb was erected in the days of King Manasseh by the priests who had fled there because of their opposition to the idolatry he practiced under Assyrian influence. It is probable that Psammeticus I agreed to this in order to ensure the loyalty of the mercenaries (1968: 386-387). They offered sacrifices there just as in the Temple in Jerusalem. But in 411 BCE it was destroyed by the Egyptians at the instigation of the priests of Khanum/Khanub the god responsible for the inundation of the Nile, whose temple was also situation in Yeb. The mercenaries appealed to Bagohi the Persian governor of Judah, and to the leadership in Judah, and even turned to the Samaritan notables to take measures to restore it. It was rebuilt in 402 BCE, after they pledged to offer only incense. This was because of Egyptian opposition to animal sacrifice, or perhaps, as Porten thinks, in order not to compete with the Temple in Jerusalem (ibid. 390). In the 4th century BCE the settlement ceased to exist for unknown reasons.

The third difference lies in the character of the leadership and organization of the migrants in Egypt. Nebuchadnezzar exiled to Babylon, together with Jehoiachin and Zedekiah, the social and spiritual leadership of Judah, leaving behind only the ordinary and poorer people who could only till the earth. After the murder of Gedaliah they were like sheep without a shepherd, and could be led in any direction; at first by Ishmael to the land of Ammon, and then by army officers to Egypt. Living in Babylon was the legal king of the House of David, Jehoiachin, with his five sons, who was granted recognition and respect also from the Babylonian authorities. The spiritual leadership was in the hands of the prophets and scribes, and the exiles maintained their communities and institutions as they had done in Judah. In contrast to them, the leaders of the remnants of Judah were Johanan the son of Kareah and the 'commanders of the tens in the field', professional soldiers, and not from the royal family or from among the ministers (such as Gedaliah's family), or scribes and prophets faithful to the laws of Moses. The shallowness of their faith is reflected in their confrontation with Jeremiah, and the biblical author even calls them הַזֵּדִים hazedim (the evil-doers). It appears that they preferred to go to Egypt since Apries, who had tried to come to the assistance of Jerusalem, was considered by them as a friend. They were also sure of finding a livelihood there as did the tens of thousands of mercenaries he employed. Under a leadership of this kind, the remnant of Judah did not set up agricultural settlements in Egypt according their origins in the homeland, as the exiles in Babylon did, but settled in places where the Saite mercenaries were stationed. Jeremiah may have witnessed their cultic rituals and also their tendency to assimilate with the local culture and religion. Greek authors have described the deep impression made by the grand temples and ceremonies conducted in Egypt on those who migrated or visited there; even the nobles and intellectuals among them felt inferior in comparison.

Like the Jews, many Greeks were forced to migrate from their homeland. According to Malkin, the colonization movement created the Greek world as a 'decentralized network'. The communities and cities in it did not have a unified starting point in place or time. They originated from different places and were formed at different times and at different sites. Most of them ascribed their founding to migration and colonization, from mother-cities in 'Old Greece' and Asia Minor, or even some of the new settlements which were founded in the areas of the Mediterranean and the Black Sea. Between the 8th and 5th centuries BCE, Greek culture was consolidated by 'convergence through divergence'. Cultic centers, temples and pan-hellenic oracles were established, the Homeric epics were disseminated, and literary and art conventions were developed. A 'confrontational' Greek identity was created against the Persians in the east and against the Phoenicians and Punics on the west (2011: 5-8). Rosen pointed out the resemblance between the Greek concept of χώρα (land, homeland) and its opposite, the ξενιτειά (living in a foreign land or in exile), and between the Hebrew concept of מְכוֹרָה mechora and its opposites פְּזוּרָה pezura and גָּלוּת galut (the word 'mechora' appears for the first time in Ezekiel. In its Sumerian-Akkadian origins as well as its evolvement into the Greek χώρα, it has the meaning of 'womb' and 'mother city'). But from the very start there exists an essential difference in their character and the attitude towards them. In the Bible, exile is perceived as a terrible punishment by heaven for the sins of the people. For this reason the concept has connotations of זַעֲוָה za'ava - horror and dread. There is an expression for this in the Septuagint for the verse 'והייתם לזעוה לכל ממלכות הארץ' (and you shalt become a thing of horror to all the kingdoms of the earth) (Deuteronomy 28: 25): Here זַעֲוָה is translated 'διασπορά'. In Greece, by contrast, migration and settlement were considered as a human initiative, and a solution to social and economic problems, and therefore had connotations of redemption and victory (2008: 43-47). Doukellis noted the opposition between διασπορά which has a negative connotation and αποικία apoikia (colonia) which has a positive meaning. It derives from οικέω/οικίζω which refer to 'home' (generally associated with the word πόλις polis). It has the positive sense of sending out citizens from the mother-city to create an autonomous new city that became for it a source of pride (2008: 97-98, 105-106). The settlements even relied on divine confirmation. Apollo Αρχηγέτης Archegetes (the founder of a colony) extended his patronage over the colonists, and they received guidelines from the cultic center in Delphi. The leader of every new settlement was called οικιστής oikistes and his cult as the founding hero was established in a ceremony for the establishment of the settlement. Thus it became a religious center in itself. The network of religious centers constituted the Greek *ecumene*, and the relations among them was multi-directional and not hierarchical (Malkin 2011: 22). The settlements maintained a special affiliation with their mother-cities (although the relation between them was not of a uniform nature, and they could range from respect and total agreement to military confrontation).

The Greeks in Egypt guarded their links to their cities of origin. Yet not only did they do so, but they formed together a collective Hellenic identity. The very remoteness from the homeland strengthened the link to it, and even created a closeness among those distant from her and stressed their resemblance (Malkin 2003: 59 'networks'). Naukratis was not a mother-city settlement which was founded under the guidance of Delphi. The Greeks received the Saites permission to settle there and also 'to set up altars and sacred sites for their gods' (Herodotus II.178). Greeks from various cities and of different origin –

Dorians, Ionians, and Aeolians – set up a common temple that was called 'Hellenion' Ἑλλήνιον (ibid.) which was discovered in the excavations of the city. Also found were dedications 'τῶν θεῶν τῶν Ἑλλήνων' (to the gods of the Greeks) (Hökmann & Möller 2006: 11-22). In the view of the above mentioned authors, its definition by Malkin as 'pan-hellenic' was more appropriate for temples such as Olympia and Delphi, but they agree with him that the Hellenion consolidated Greek identity as against the surrounding Egyptians (ibid. 17-18). In Memphis as well, the Carian mercenaries who had apparently arrived from different cities in Caria, erected a common temple in their neighborhood which was called 'Καρικον'. Malkin points to another factor for the consolidation of the Greeks: the Egyptian perception of them as a collective entity called 'WJNN' (derived from Ionia, like the Hebrew 'Yavan' in the Bible). For example, the mercenaries who engraved their names on the foot of the statue of Rameses II in Abu Simbel (apparently during the period of Psammeticus II). They came from various cities in the Aegean world, and belonged to a unit called αλλογλοσσοι (foreign speakers); it is reasonable to suppose that this was the epithet given them by the Egyptians and not by themselves (2003: 92 'Pan-Hellenism').

On the other hand, the Egyptian cultural and religious influence on the Aegean migrants was profound. The Egyptians persuaded the Greeks who came to their country as tourists and migrants, that they were superior to them in the antiquity of their culture and cultic rituals. According to Plato, the priest in the temple of Neith in Sais told Solon, the Athenian lawgiver who visited there about the year 570 BCE, that the Greeks were as young as children since they do not remember anything of their history before the Flood. He told him about the history of Atlantis, Egypt and Athens (*Timaeus* 23.b-25.a). Herodotus also drew his knowledge about Egypt from Egyptian priests. Even if he sometimes doubted the veracity of their stories, the 'Herodotian attitude' that embedded in Greek narrative and preserved even during the Roman period, praised the achievements of Egyptian culture, in its style of government and laws, in economy and agriculture, in the sciences and in wisdom literature. The Egyptians were credited with the inventions of wine production and irrigation canals, land measurement, and their equal allocation to the inhabitants, and as a result of this, the sciences of geometry and mathematics, astronomy and astrology, the calendar and the alphabet. Egyptian priests claimed that many Greek intellectuals and artists had stayed and studied in Egypt, such as Orpheus, Daedalus, Homer, Lycurgus, Solon, Plato, Pythagoras, Eudoxus, and Democritus of Abdera. The priests said that all their achievements, for which they were admired among the Greeks were transferred from Egypt (Diodorus I.69, 96-98). Also widely spread were the myths that ascribed to Egypt the founding of Greek cities such as Athens, Thebes, and Argos. Danaus, the ancestor of the Dorians, was thought by Herodotus to be an Egyptian, the brother of Aegyptus. Yet Greeks developed a counter-trend of criticism and scorn for Egypt, especially for its strange cults such as the sacredness of animals, circumcision, and the prohibition against pork. They also attacked its isolationism and hatred of foreigners, and the promiscuity and worthlessness of the Egyptians as warriors. They also claimed that it was the Greeks who found cities in Egypt. According to Aeschylus, Aegyptus and Danaus were the sons of Epaphus, the son of Zeus and Io, the priestess of Hera in Argos (*Suppliant Women,* 40-48) (Berthelot 1999: 192-196; Isaac 2004: 352-370). The Egyptians allowed the foreigners to participate in the mysteries of Isis, and Herodotus tells about the devout religious adherence of the Carians who took part in them. Although he was a half-Carian, Herodotus describes with derision their exaggerated and barbaric piety: 'While the Egyptians keep the feast of Isis at Busiris. There, after the sacrifice, all the men and women lament, Carians who live in Egypt do even more than this, inasmuch as they cut their foreheads with knives; and by this they show that they are foreigners and not Egyptians' (II.61). The desire to become assimilated did not help the mercenaries but only made them the object of mockery for Egypt. Even Jeremiah claimed that the Jews who observed the local cultic rituals were always considered as strangers and inferior, and were 'a curse and a reproach' in the spirit of Moses' prophecy: '…and there shalt thou serve other gods, of wood and stone. And thou shalt become an astonishment, a proverb, and a byword, among all athe nations whither the Lord shall lead thee' (Deuteronomy 28: 36-37). The opposition of Jeremiah and Herodotus to the imitations of Egyptian cultic rituals reflects their view that one should not degrade oneself before them. The Egyptians, like the Babylonians, took pride in their antiquity and culture and regarded them as a sign of their superiority to other nations. But the Jews and the Greeks also regarded themselves as the most superior of all nations. The former because they were chosen by the One God, and the latter because of their freedom and their political and social institutions.

Rosen points to the process in which the loyalty of the migrants to the new 'homeland' overpowers their affiliation with their native origins and it becomes their own homeland. The open attitude towards their new surroundings and the readiness to become assimilated within it is greater among the migrants by their own free will. The commander of the mercenaries in Abu Simbel was called Psammeticus the son of Theocles. His father was apparently among the first generation of migrants, and gave his son the Egyptian name of the king his patron. Archaeological evidence indicates the depth of the influence of Egyptian culture on the Greeks that arrived there (Villing & Schlotzhauer 2006: 5-8). The Carians who lived in Memphis were called during the Persian period 'καρομέμφεται' as if they had created a new nationality and were different from their Carian brethren (Ray 2003: 192). They lived in a quarter called 'Καρικον'. In the necropolis to the north of Saqqara, cultic statues and tomb monuments were found with inscriptions in the Carian and Egyptian languages, and with burial scenes according to Egyptian conventions (Yoyotte & Masson 1956; Ray 2003) **(Fig. 19)**. The many gift offerings dedicated by the Carians were made of bronze, imbued with mystic-military significance. Carians and Egyptians lived in Babylon since the time of Nebuchadnezzar, and it seems that he had brought them as captives when he returned from his military campaign against Egypt. Even there, they lived in close company with each other and documents mention them together (Zadok 2005: 81-84). The Ionians in Memphis lived in the 'Ελλήνιον' quarter, north of 'Καρικον' with their own temple, and were called 'Ελληνομέμφεται' (*PSI* 488.12. PCair.Zen. 59593.7-8; Thompson 1988: 83-84, 95-97, notes 7-9, 70-77). The Ionians were especially devoted to the cult of Apis (which recalls the prophecy of Jeremiah on the fatted calf). A Helenomemphite Papyrus of the end of the 4th century BCE can indicate that they originated from the mercenaries of Amasis. It deals with the trial that was conducted by Artemisia, daughter of Amasis, calling as witness the god Serapis. An example of the cultural syncretism is a black-figured amphora, which was created in Ionia, and its fragments were found in Thebes (biblical name: No-Amon). It is called in research the 'Apries Amphora', since it bears the cartouches of Apries. It

FIG. 19. CARIAN STELA FROM SAQQARA.
ROUND-TOPPED LIMESTONE STELA. DATE: 30TH DYNASTY. FINDSPOT: SAQQARA, H5-1343, MEMPHIS, EGYPT. THE BRITISH MUSEUM, NO. EA67235. © THE TRUSTEES OF THE BRITISH MUSEUM.
STELA WITH INCISED DETAIL DIVIDED INTO THREE REGISTERS: 1. MALE FIGURE BEFORE OSIRIS AND ISIS. 2. IBIS-HEADED FIGURE BEFORE A BULL; CARIAN TEXT ABOVE. 3. DECEASED WOMAN ON COUCH WITH MOURNERS.

FIG. 20. IONIAN AMPHORA FROM THEBES.
POTTERY AMPHORA, FRAGMENTARY, WITH PAINTED DECORATION. MADE IN: NORTH IONIA, ASIA MINOR (TURKEY). DATE: 6TH CENTURY BCE. FINDSPOT: THEBES (NO-AMON), EGYPT. THE BRITISH MUSEUM, NO. 2006,L01.1. © The Trustees of the British Museum.
ON ONE SIDE CONFRONTED BOXERS FLANK A PRIZE DINOS ON A STAND; A BIRD, PROBABLY A RAPTOR, STANDING ON AN IONIC COLUMN, SURVIVES BEHIND ONE OF THE BOXERS. ON THE OTHER SIDE THE HEADS OF TWO STANDING WOMEN REMAIN, BEHIND WHOM ARE PLANTS, A TREE OR A BUSH. ONLY ONE HANDLE IS PRESENT AND THE LOWER BODY IS ALMOST COMPLETELY GONE, TOGETHER WITH THE BASE. AROUND THE NECK OF THE VASE IS A BAND OF FOUR CARTOUCHES WITH THE THRONE NAME AND THE BIRTH NAME OF THE EGYPTIAN KING APRIES OF THE SAITE DYNASTY.

describes a fight between two boxers and a bird standing on an Ionic column (Bailey 2006: 155-157) **(Fig. 20)**. The Greeks settled in the Saite fortress in Tell el-Heir, which is Migdol, during the Persian period also adopted Egyptian burial customs (Oren 1992: 1111-1112).

It seems that a new date, place and motive should be proposed for the compilation of the story of the duel between David and Goliath. It was consolidated in a number of stages. Its ancient sources were apparently edited during the reign of Josiah. Later it solidified among the opponents of the alliance between Jehoiakim, Jehoiachin and Zedekiah and the Saites. But its importance was especially emphasized after the destruction. Its message was not directed at the Jews in Babylon or Judah but at the diaspora in Egypt, in its early days when it was led by military officers to the cities of the mercenaries and settled there with the permission of the Saites. Many of them found employment as mercenaries, and became intimately familiar with the Aegean way of life, cults and ethos. Then the urgent need arose to prevent their assimilation. The dread of assimilation is reflected in the stories of Sisra and Goliath, as prophecies that mocked the Saites and their mercenaries and as prophecies of anger against the polytheistic remnant of Judah. The message was that these were the enemies of Israel and its God. Another lesson to be learnt from the story for Jews in Egypt was that in spite of their 'underdog' status, they should not feel inferior to the other mercenaries and imitate them through self-abnegation. The literary-psychological means were the ridicule in the comic scenes of the arrogant 'general of the armies' descending from his chariot in flight, and killed in his sleep by a woman. And of the 'armored' and boastful giant who is felled to the ground by a small shepherd boy. In the ideological battle against the Saites and the Aegeans, the Bible makes skillful use of motifs and ideas taken from their world and culture with which the Jews had become familiar through their contact and friction with them, first as conquered vassals and then as allies, for nearly a hundred years before they came to Egypt as migrants in search of refuge.

Why was the message transmitted in a coded and allegorical form? Because the Jews were residing in Egypt as migrants seeking refuge and protection, and were dependent upon the good will of the Saites rulers. They also obtained their livelihood as their mercenaries… only Jeremiah dared to attack them openly just as he had formerly attacked Jehoiakim and Zedekiah in Judah. The prophecies to the mercenaries in the Book of Jeremiah also should be dated to his lifetime.[25]

The need for ethnic separation and cultic purification as a means for survival as an exiled minority was stressed also in the Babylonian exile. During the days of the Return to Zion this also was required in Judah because of the many intermarriages, and Ezra and Nehemiah forced the people to divorce their foreign wives with their children who did not speak the Judaean language (Hebrew) but 'half-Ashdodite' (Nehemiah 13: 24). This

---

[25] Scholars have noted the resemblance between the style of the prose sections in the Book of Jeremiah and the style of Deuteronomy, Joshua, Judges, Samuel and Kings. They believe that they were not written but by the Deut. authors after him (Nicholson 1975: 10-16). Hoffman attributes the biographical and historiographical sections in Jeremiah to a late editor. Jehoiachin was released from prison in 561 BCE (Jeremiah 52: 31-34), and matters such as the release of slaves and Sabbath day observance in Chapters 17 and 34 are appropriate for the time of Ezra. This means that the editing process continued until the mid-5th century BCE (2001: 62-68, 77-78).

produced results, and in the period after the destruction of the First Temple, monotheism strengthened in the Jewish faith (Judaism). Hoffman indicates the gradual development of monotheism in Israel (as against the approach of Y. Kaufman, on one hand, who believes it was monotheistic from the beginning, and the approach of N. P. Lemche following J. Wellhausen, on the other hand, that it was polytheistic until the period of the Return to Zion). In the Deut. literature before the Second Isaiah, there are monotheistic declarations such as 'Hear O Israel: The Lord our God, the Lord is one', but side by side there is also the recognition of the existence of other gods, although weak in power, and frequent warnings against worshipping them. In Jeremiah as well, there is the expression 'foreign gods', and as opposed to God who is the 'source of living waters', they are 'broken cisterns that can hold no water' (Jeremiah 2: 13). They have no power to help Israel. But in the Second Isaiah, at the beginning of the Return to Zion, monotheism is already absolute: 'I am the first, and I am the last; and beside me there is no God' (ibid. 44: 6), and: 'To whom then will ye liken me, or shall I be equal?' (ibid. 40: 25).

Conclusion

To summarize, let us go back to the conflicting approaches towards the ethos of the hoplite protective equipment. Homer stresses time and again its effectiveness and paralyzing impression. 'The arms of Achilles… rang aloud in their splendour. Then trembling seized all the Myrmidons, neither dared any man to look thereon, but they shrank in fear' *(Iliad* XIX: 13-16). 'His shield and helmet shone and went afar gleams as they were the moon and morning star' (ibid. XIX: 374-382). 'And the battle… bristled with long spears … and eyes were blinded by the blaze of bronze from gleaming helmets, and corselets newly burnished, and shining shields' (ibid. XIII: 338-343). Alcaeus, of the same generation as Jeremiah, relates in one of his poems about the house 'dedicated to Ares' in which the floor, walls and even ceiling were covered with bronze helmets, greaves and shields, armor made of linen, and swords. He delighted to look at the beauty and polished brightness of the shining weapons. When the Bible describes in detail the Greek metal weapons it does so to denigrate their futility and worthlessness against the God of Israel.

The Bible stresses the prohibition against making any statue or image of God: '… for ye saw no manner of similitude on the day that the Lord spoke unto you in Horeb out of the midst of the fire' (Deuteronomy 4: 15). Yet it does bring descriptions of God at various levels of concretization. The voice of God speaks to Moses from within the burning bush. According to Psalms 104: 2 he covers himself 'with light as with a garment' and stretches 'the heavens like a curtain'. Isaiah the son of Amoz describes God seated in a temple filled with the hems of his robes: 'I saw also the Lord sitting upon a throne, high and lifted up, and his train filled the temple' (Isaiah 6: 1). But the most concrete imaging seems to be found in no other than the Second Isaiah. He is the one who mocks those who fashion their gods from wood that also serves them for heating and cooking (ibid. 44: 15-17); who stresses more than any other source in the Bible the absence of any iconography for God and the worthlessness of matter: 'To whom then will ye liken God? or what likeness will ye compare unto him? The workman melteth a graven image, and the goldsmith spreadeth it over with gold, and casteth silver chains. He that is so impoverished that he had no oblation chooseth a tree that will not rot; he seeketh unto him a cunning workman to prepare a graven image, that shall not be moved … To whom then will ye liken me, or shall I be equal? saith the Holy One' (ibid. 40: 18-20, 25). The Second Isaiah describes how God dresses in the full armor of the hoplite and goes out to war against his enemies: 'For he put on righteousness as a breastplate, and an helmet of salvation upon his head; and he put on the garments of vengeance for clothing and was clad with zeal as a cloak' (ibid. 59: 17). For a moment we are astonished at the forbidden imagery, and even more so in the form of the armored hoplite enemy. But at second glance it becomes clear that this was merely a literary device, and the details about arms are not real and concrete but a metaphor for the abstract concepts of righteousness, salvation, vengeance and zeal. As in the story of David and Goliath, God adopts the very means of his opponent to vanquish him with his own weapons.

The end of the Saite dynasty and its mercenaries came in 525 BCE through Cambyses. It seems that this was the background to the call by Zechariah the prophet who was active in

Judah from the year 520 BCE: 'Rejoice greatly, O daughter of Zion ... When I have bent Judah for me, filled the bow with Ephraim, and raised up thy sons, O Zion, against thy sons, O Greece, and made thee as the sword of a mighty man. ...The Lord of hosts shall defend them; and they shall devour, and subdue with sling stones ...And the Lord their God shall save them in that day as the flock of his people' (Zechariah 9: 9-16). This time God goes out to battle like the shepherd protecting his flock, and the sons of Zion are in his hands like a bow, a sword, and sling stones.

The time, place and circumstances for the basis of the duel story derived from ancient sources were firstly in Judah, in view of the opposition of the Deut. circles to the influence of Saite Egypt on the policies of Josiah's heirs. But it was given greater stress after the destruction with the migration of the 'remnant of Judah' under the leadership of army commanders to Egypt. It reflects the fears among those circles of the return to idolatry which had preceded the time of Josiah under the strong impression made upon the people by the Egyptian temples and cults ('the monuments of Beth shemesh'), by the tens of thousands of Aegean mercenaries with their shining bronze armor, so proud of themselves, on whom the Egyptian empire was dependent. The Jews had already been familiar with them during the 7th century BCE, firstly as conquerors and forces stationed in service of the Saites, and later on as an allied army against Babylon. In the end they became their neighbors in Egypt, earning their livelihood like them as mercenaries. It was then that ethnic, military and government administration terms from Aegean sources were introduced into the Bible, such as: Ἰωνίη/יָוָן Yavan, Ἀχαιος/אָכִישׁ Achish, γιαλαθώραξ/גָּלְיָת Goliath, κύμβαχος/כּוֹבָע kova, πέλθε/פלת׳ Plethi, συστράτηγος/סִיסְרָא sisra, εγχειριδίον/כִּדוֹן kidon, ἄναξ/עֲנָק anak, τύραννοι/סְרָנִים sranim. Some of the terms were used ironically against the influence of the Greek ethos that contradicted the Deut. spirit. The message of the story was that they should be regarded as sworn enemies and should be kept apart. The aim was also to strengthen loyalty to the House of David. It employs the psychological warfare of distorted motifs taken from familiar Greek and Egyptian narratives and ridicule of the Aegean-Saite military ethos. The prophets use a similar irony in the terms taken from Egyptian wisdom literature as well as the Saite myths and ethos as a tool against their political and religious influence.

Contrary to the prophecy of Jeremiah, that the Jews of Egypt would be destroyed, their numbers grew, and their migration from Judah continued even during the Persian and Ptolemaic periods because of economic distress. Rofé points out the expression of fear in the Bible that the land was being emptied of Jews (Genesis 24: 5, 8; Ezekiel 34; Nehemiah 5; and in Ben-Sira (Rofé 1986: 3-10). From archaeological research it appears that the Return to Zion was not very large in scope as it is described in Ezra and Nehemiah, and that many preferred to remain in Babylon. No archaeological evidence was found for construction projects in Judah during the Persian period. Its material culture was poor and it was a continuation of that which prevailed during the Babylonian period. There were no urban centers and the number of inhabitants was estimated at only 12,000 approximately. Demographic and urban transformation occurred only during the Hellenistic period (Wiesehöfer 2011; Lipshitz 2011; Finkelstein 2011). Apparently this was also the reason why the spiritual leadership in Babylon and Judah did not take a favorable view of the Egyptian diaspora which was growing larger at the expense of the population in Judah.

According to The *Letter of Aristeas*, Jews arrived in Egypt after the Persian conquest. But it was Ptolemy I who made a particular contribution to the increase in their numbers by bringing a hundred thousand Jews from the Land of Israel after he conquered it (in 301 BCE). Those of them who were young and well trained in weapons, thirty thousand men, he armed and settled as stationary forces in the districts of Egypt, and the rest he enslaved for a while (*Aristeas*, 13-14). The Jews offered their military services to the Macedonian conquerors, as they had previously done to the Saites and Persians before them. They attained military and economic power and had much influence in the royal court. In the cities where they resided they received civil rights equal to the Greek citizens. According to Kasher, this was in recompense for their military services (2008: 122-125). They adopted the Greek language into which they translated the Bible, and also Greek cultural values (according to Aristeas some of the translators had Greek names and had studied carefully Greek literature). They tried to give an official religious and legal approval for their diaspora existence, in view of the prohibition in the Torah and Prophets to reside in Egypt. Josephus quotes the story of Hecataeus of Abdera (an ethnographer of the 4th century BCE), that Hezekiah, the high priest of the Jews, settled in Egypt during the reign of Ptolemy I. In front of those who came with him he read out a complete scroll that contained the story of their settlement and their laws (*Against Apion*, I, 186-189). Bar-Kokhba and others call the author 'pseudo-Hecataeus' and believe he was a Jewish Egyptian who lived at the end of the 1st century BCE. In addition, they tried to give their diaspora a legitimacy in the eyes of the Greeks and Romans by comparing it to the Greek settlement movement. In the Septuagint the word גלות (exile) is translated as αποικία (Mélèze Modrzejewski 1993: 70-80). A comparison of this kind was also made by Philo the Alexandrian. In his view, Jerusalem, the eternal holy city and the center of Jewish existence, is the metropolis that sent them into the diaspora. But they loved and were loyal everywhere to their πατρίς (the fatherland) in which they had been born and raised. He claimed that the Jews had migrated to these places and had existed there from the moment they were established (*Philo's Flaccus*, 138-140). (But Jews, of course, had never founded independent settlements like the Greeks).

Yet the Jews did not become assimilated in Egypt. Even the Jews of Yeb, believers in Anath-Yahu, maintained their separation from the non-Jews. According to their documents, the Egyptian influence through mixed marriages and cultic practices was minimal. In spite of the commandment for exclusive cultic rites in Jerusalem, the religious leadership in Jerusalem was interested in keeping them from becoming assimilated. It assisted them in restoring their temple and guided them in the laws for the Passover.

The second Jewish temple of the Egyptian Jews is known in rabbinical literature as the 'House of Onias', which was erected around the mid-2nd century BCE. This time it was founded by the head of the Jewish spiritual leadership himself, the deposed High Priest Onias of the house of Zadok, who went down to Egypt. He persuaded Ptolemy VI Philom128 (180-145 BCE) that the temple would unify the scattered Jews of Egypt and strengthen their loyalty to the regime. The spiritual leadership in Judah was divided in their opinion about him. Some of the Tannaim defined this as idolatry, but others even permitted the offering of sacrifices in the temple.[26]

---

[26] The Temple of Onias was located in Leontopolis in the Heliopolis district in Egypt. According to Josephus,

CONCLUSION

The self-identity and faith of the Jews of Egypt was preserved after they had internalized the message of the prophets and of Deut. historiography thanks to the constant stream of migrants from Judah, in which the national consolidation and cultic purification of Ezra and Nehemiah had succeeded, and as a result of pride in Hasmonaean political power. But this was also a reaction to external pressure, the tensions and violent confrontations they

---

it was erected by Onias III (*War of the Jews* VII, 10.12) Or Onias IV (*Antiquities* XIII, 62-73) who fled from Jerusalem. He was not prompted by honest intentions but by the desire for honor and anger at the Temple in Jerusalem. He claimed in the presence of Ptolemy that the new temple would led to the unification of cultic practices among the Jews in Egypt, and ensure their loyalty to the regime. According to Schwartz, this was an ironic statement by Josephus since, as he says, Ptolemy and his wife were surprised at his choice of an idolatrous site in Bubastis which was filled with animals sacred to the Egyptians. From rabbinical sources it appears that the spiritual leadership in Judah was divided about him. Some of the Tannaim after the destruction of the Second Temple permitted sacrifices to be offered and vows to be made in it, while others compared the priests to those of idol worshippers (Babylonian Talmud, 'Menahot' 109b; Jerusalem Talmud, 'Yoma' 6, 33). In any case, the Temple of Onias was not mentioned in Jewish Hellenistic literature which was mostly composed in Egypt. Scholars differ in their opinion about the reason for this. Safrai thinks that it served only the settlement of mercenaries in an isolated district of Heliopolis (1965: 63). Kasher is of the opinion that it did not compete with the Temple in Jerusalem but only served the Jews in the 'Land of Onias' (1995: 80). According to Yankelewitz it did not occupy any real place in the world of Second Temple Jewry. The Tannaite controversy over it took place after the Bar Kokhba revolt, and was merely of academic interest. It reflected approaches towards religious centers in the diaspora that encroached upon the hegemony of the leadership in the Land of Israel (1993: 107-115). But in the view of Schwartz, archaeological finds and foreign sources such as Strabo (quoted in *Antiquities*, XIV, 117) show that the Land of Onias was central for Egyptian Jewry, and contained a temple. Schwartz explains his words as follows: 'In Egypt, from the country (chora) a settlement (katoikia) of the Jews was set apart, while from the city of the Alexandrians a large part was assigned for this people' (and not that the settlement was set apart from the city of Alexandria). This was the settlement referred to by Josephus in *Antiquities*, XIV, 131: 'The Jews that dwelt τὴν Ὀνίου λεγομένην χώραν κατοικοῦντες (in the land called the Land of Onias) '. This means that there were two large Jewish centers in Egypt, in Alexandria and in the Land of Onias. But there is no direct reference to the Temple of Onias in Hellenistic literature because the Jews in Egypt were not interested in the temple cult - whether in Leontopolis or in Jerusalem - but focused on synagogues and prayers (1997: 22). Josephus and the rabbinical sages relate that Onias based his action on Isaiah 19: 18-19: 'In that day shall five cities in the land of Egypt speak the language of Canaan, and swear to the Lord of hosts; one shall be called, 'עִיר הַהֶרֶס' ('The city of destruction'). In that day shall there be an altar to the Lord in the midst of the land of Egypt, and a pillar at the border thereof to the Lord'. 'The city of destruction' is an intentional distortion by the MT of the original version, which is known to us from the Isaiah scrolls of Qumran 'עִיר הַחֶרֶס' ('the city of the sun', Heliopolis); So is it in the Latin translation of the Vulgate: *civitas soli*. This is the 'Bethshemesh' (the city of the sun) of Jeremiah, who prophesied the destruction of its idolatrous monuments. Schwartz points out that in the Septuagint the term is translated as 'city of righteousness', which reflects the positive view of Egyptian Jewry of this city (ibid. 14-16). The erection of the Temple of Onias is not mentioned also in the book of 2 *Maccabees*, which presents Onias with acclaim (2 *Maccabees* is an abridgment of the 5-volums book by Jason of Cyrene, composed in Greek for the Jews of the diaspora, while 1 *Maccabees* was composed in the Land of Israel, in Hebrew). Schwartz infers from this that the book was composed before the erection of the temple, otherwise a strong opposition to the temple would have been expressed in it. But perhaps this can be regarded in a different light because of the story it mentions about the vision of Judah the Maccabee before his victory over Nicanor: 'Judah [spoke] to his own and armed every one of them, not with the weapons of shield and spear, but with the best speeches and exhortations; and he explained to them a dream… in which he rejoiced with them all: Onias, who had been high priest, a good and kind man, modest…trained in the virtues, extending his hands, praying for the safety of the people of the Jews. After this, here appeared also another man, admirable in age and glory, and with a bearing of great dignity about him. Onias said: 'This one loves his brothers and the people of Israel. This is he who prays greatly for the people and for all the holy city: Jeremiah, the prophet of God.' Then Jeremiah extended his right hand, and he gave to Judas a sword of gold, saying: 'Receive this holy sword as a gift from God, with it you shall cast down the adversaries of my people Israel'' (2 *Maccabees* 15: 11-16). Perhaps the indirect message of the story is that there is heavenly agreement for the transfer of the high priesthood from the House of Zadok, which had held it since the days of King David, to the House of the Hasmonaeans. Another message was that one should not fear that the Temple of Onias would take over the place or harm the status of the Temple in Jerusalem. This is with the confirmation of the greatest of opponents to the migration to Egypt, who had foretold the destruction of the temples in Heliopolis. It is reasonable to suppose that the Hasmonaeans would be interested to have the Zadok family go down to Egypt and vacate their role to them.

had with the Egyptians and Greeks. Bar-Kokhba found the sources for the anti-Semitic fabrications that appeared in Greek literature during the Classical and Hellenistic periods, such as the cult of the ass head in the Temple in Jerusalem, the exodus of lepers from Egypt, and blood libels – in the stories that the Egyptian priests and scribes had woven during the Persian period (2010: 238-243, 255-275, 313-323, 327-337). The Jews served as mercenaries for the Persians who had conquered Egypt and Asia Minor, and were hated by both the Egyptians and the Greeks. In addition, the cultic practices and national-historical narratives of the Jews and the Egyptians were opposed, and were perceived by each side as loathsome and provocative. The Jews hated the cult of heavenly bodies, animals, and the deification of Pharaoh among the Egyptians. The animal sacrifices of the Jews and the annual celebration of the Passover which included the sacrifice of a ram in which the main Egyptian god Amun was incarnated, and their stories of the plagues of Egypt and the drowning of Pharaoh and his army in the sea, angered and humiliated the Egyptians. They invented as a counter-narrative of the 'exodus of the lepers', which reflects the Jewish narrative like a distorting mirror. For this purpose they borrowed and twisted many motifs from the Bible. One version tells about the Jews in Egypt who were afflicted with the plague of pestilence and boils which they spread among the Egyptians. Pharaoh inquired of the god Amun through the oracle and was commanded to drown the Jews in the sea. A second version says that the community of unbelievers in the gods caused a drought in Egypt until the oracle of Amun ordered that they should be banished to the desert, where Moses formed them into a people and led them to Jerusalem. They based this on the story of the hand of Moses struck by leprosy and of Miriam becoming leprous (Exodus 4: 6; Numbers 12: 1-3). Greek authors improved on the stories and disseminated them both in the Seleucid royal court during the days of Antiochus IV Epiphanes (175-164 BCE) and in Egypt. The political and military influence of the Jews in the Ptolemaic royal court increased during the reign of Cleopatra II (185-116 BCE), and Cleopatra III (161-101 BCE). This aroused the jealousy and fears of the Greeks in Egypt who felt rejected and betrayed by the Macedonian rulers. Therefore they supported Ptolemy Lathyros, the son of Cleopatra III who rebelled against her. Consequently, Lysimachus of Alexandria, who had fabricated the leper story, tried to break all contact between the Pharaohs and Greece. Contrary to the tradition that attributed the founding of Thebes in Boeotia to Egypt, he revived the classical myth that attributed it to Cadmus of Tyre. Philo relates that the hatred against the Jews was deeply rooted in the Egyptian people. It broke out during the days of Caligula in the pogroms that the Egyptians and Greeks carried out against the Jews of Alexandria. The Jews of Egypt assisted the rebels in Judah during the time of the Great Revolt (66-70 CE), after which many of the *sicarii*, extremist Jewish Zealots, fled to Egypt. In 73 CE, three years after the Temple in Jerusalem was destroyed, Vespasian closed the Temple of Onias (*War of the Jews*, VII, 421).

Bibliography

A. Literary sources and commentaries

Aeschylus, 'Suppliant Women'. *Aeschylus*, in 2 volumes. Vol. 2, with an English translation by H. W. Smyth, Cambridge, MA, Harvard University Press; London, William Heinemann, Ltd., 1926.

Ammianus Marcellinus, *Rerum Gestarum*, with an English Translation by J. C. Rolfe, Cambridge, MA, Harvard University Press; London, William Heinemann, Ltd., 1935-1940.

ANET-Ancient Near Eastern Texts Relating to The Old Testament, ed. J. B. Pritchard, Princeton, NJ, Princeton University Press, 1950.

Anthologia Lirica Graeca, ed. E. Diehl, Lipsiae, Teubneri, 1949.

Archilochus, *Elegy and Iambus*, Vol. II, 2, with an English translation by J. M. Edmonds, Cambridge, MA, Harvard University Press; London, William Heinemann Ltd., 1931.

Aristeas, *The Letter Of Aristeas*, ed. R.H. Charles, Oxford, Clarendon Press, 1913.

Aristophanes, 'Acharneians', 'Peace'. *Aristophanes Comoediae*, eds. F. W. Hall & W. M. Geldart, Vol. 1, Oxford, Clarendon Press, 1907. (Greek).

Aristophanes, 'Acharnians'. *The Eleven Comedies*. Anonymous, New York. Liveright. N.P.Y.

Cornelius Nepos, 'Timotheus'. *Vitae*. A. Fleckeisen, Leipzig, Teubner, 1886.

The Book of 2 Maccabees, with a Hebrew introduction, translation and explanation by D. Shwartz, Jerusalem, Yad izhak ben-zvi, 2004.

Demosthenes, 'Against Aristocrates'. *Demosthenes*, with an English translation by A. T. Murray, Cambridge, MA, Harvard University Press; London, William Heinemann Ltd, 1939.

Diodorus Siculus, *Diodori Bibliotheca Historica*, Vol 1-2. Immanuel Bekker. Ludwig Dindorf. Friedrich Vogel. Leipzig, Teubner, 1888-1890.

Diodorus Siculus, Burton, A., *Diodorus Siculus Book I: a Commentary*, Leiden, Brill, 1972.

Diogenes Laertius, 'Life of Pittacus', *Lives of Eminent Philosophers*, translated by R. D. Hicks, Cambridge, MA, Harvard University Press, 1972 (First published 1925).

Euripides, 'Bacchae'. *The Tragedies of Euripides*, translated by T. A. Buckley, London, H. G. Bohn, 1850.

Greek Lyric 1: Sappho and Alcaeus, ed. D. A. Campbell, Cambridge, Mass., 1982. http://www.scribd.com/doc/34720745/Sappho-and-Alcaeus-Loeb.

Flavius Josephus, *Antiquities of the Jews*. Books 1-VI. Translated into Hebrew by A. Shalit, Jerusalem, Reuven Mas, 1985.

Flavius Josephus, *The Wars of the Jews*. Translated into Hebrew by S. Hagai, Jerusalem, Reuven Mas, 1964.

Herodotus, with an English translation by A. D. Godley. Cambridge, MA, Harvard University Press; London, William Heinemann Ltd., 1926.

Hesiod, 'Theogony'. *The Homeric Hymns and Homerica* with an English Translation by H. G. Evelyn-White, Cambridge, MA, Harvard University Press; London, William Heinemann Ltd., 1914.

Homer, *Homeri Opera* in 5 volumes, Oxford, Oxford University Press, 1920.

Homer, *The Iliad* in 2 volumes with an English Translation by A.T. Murray, Cambridge, MA, Harvard University Press, London, William Heinemann Ltd.,1924.

Isocrates, *Isocrates* in 3 volumes with an English Translation by G. Norlin, Cambridge, MA, Harvard University Press; London, William Heinemann Ltd., 1980.

Lexicon of Ancient Greek Language, I. Stamatakos, Athens, Phoenix, 1972. (Greek).

Pausanias, *Pausaniae Graeciae Descriptio*, 3 Vols. Leipzig, Teubner, 1903.

Pausanias, *Pausanias Description of Greece*, in 4 Volumes with an English Translation by W.H. S. Jones & H. A. Ormerod, Cambridge, MA, Harvard University Press; London, William Heinemann Ltd., 1918.

Philo's Flaccus, the first pogrom. introduction, translation, and commentary by P. W. van der Horst, Leiden, Brill, 2003.

Plato, *Platonis Opera*, ed. J. Burnet, Oxford, Oxford University Press, 1903. (Greek).

Plato, 'Laches'. *Plato,* in 12 Volumes, Vol. 8 translated by W. R. M. Lamb, Cambridge, MA, Harvard University Press; London, William Heinemann Ltd., 1955.

Plato, 'Timaeus'. *Plato,* in 12 Volumes, Vol. 9 translated by W. R. M. Lamb, Cambridge, MA, Harvard University Press; London, William Heinemann Ltd., 1925.

Plato, 'Laws'. *Plato,* in 12 Volumes, Vols. 10 & 11 translated by R. G. Burry, Cambridge, MA, Harvard University Press; London, William Heinemann Ltd., 1967 & 1968.

Plato, 'Republic'. *Plato,* in 12 Volumes, Vols. 5 & 6 translated by P. Shorey, Cambridge, MA, Harvard University Press; London, William Heinemann Ltd., 1968.

Plutarch, *Moralia*, in 15 Volumes, Vol. 3 translated by F. C. Babbit, Cambridge, MA, Harvard University Press; London, William Heinemann Ltd., 1931.

Plutarch, 'Demetrius'. *The Parallel Lives*, Vol. IX, with an English Translation by B. Perrin. Cambridge, MA, Harvard University Press; London, William Heinemann Ltd. 1920.

Plutarch, 'Pelopidas'. *The Parallel Lives*, Vol. V, with an English Translation by B. Perrin. Cambridge, MA, Harvard University Press; London, William Heinemann Ltd. 1917. 5.

Plutarch, 'Philopoemen'. *The Parallel Lives*, Vol. X, with an English Translation by B. Perrin. Cambridge, MA, Harvard University Press; London, William Heinemann Ltd. 1921.

Polyaenus, *Stratagems*, Adapted from the translation by R. Shepherd, London, 1793, book 1, Chapters 1-26, *www.attalus.org/translate/polyaenus1A.htm*

Strabo, *The Geography of Strabo*. ed. H. L. Jones, Cambridge, MA; London, William Heinemann Ltd., 1924.

Strabo, *Geographica*, ed. A. Meineke, Leipzig, Teubner, 1877.

Thucydides, *The Peloponnesian War,* translated by R. Crawley, London. J. M. Dent; New York, E. P. Dutton, 1910.

Tyrtaeus, *The Elegiac Poems of Tyrtaeus. Elegy and Iambus*, with an English Translation by. J. M. Edmonds, Cambridge, MA; London, William Heinemann Ltd, 1931. http://www.perseus.tufts.edu/hopper/text?doc=Perseus%3Atext%3A2008.01.0477%3Avolume%3D1%3Atext%3D2%3Asection%3D2

Xenophon, 'Anabasis'. *Xenophontis opera Omnia*, ed. E. C. Marchant, Vol. 3, Oxford, Clarendon Press, 1904. (repr. 1961).

Xenophon, 'Hellenica'. *Xenophon,* in 7 Volumes, Vol. 1 & 2, translated by C. L. Brownson, Cambridge, MA; London, William Heinemann, Ltd., 1918; 1921.

B. Modern studies

Asimakopoulos, S. 'The Armament of the Ancient Greeks', (1-4), *Archaiologia kai Technes*, 1994, no. 50: 113-114, no. 51: 113-114, no. 52: 105-106, Vol. 53: 105-106. (Greek).

Aharoni, Y. 'The Arad Ostraca', *Qadmoniot*, Vol. 1, no. 3, 1968, pp. 101-103. (Hebrew).

Aharoni, Y., *Arad Inscriptions*, 1981.

Amit, Y., *The Book of Judges: The Art of Editing*, 1992. (Hebrew).

Arieli, Y., *History and Politics*, 1992. (Hebrew).

Bailey, D., 'The Apries Amphora – Another Cartouche', in: Villing, A., & Schlotzhauer, U., (eds.), pp. 155-157.

Bar-Kokhva, B., *The Image of the Jews in Greek Literature: The Hellenistic Period*, 2010.

Ben Yosef Tawil, H., *An Akkadian Lexical Companion For Biblical Hebrew*, 2009.

Bekker-Nielsen, T., & Hannestad, L., (eds.), *War as a Cultural and Social Force: Essays on Warfare in Antiquity*, 2001.

Bernabé, A., 'El Vocabolario de las Armas en Micénico', *Gladius*, Vol. XXVII, 2007, pp. 15-38.

Bernand, A. & Masson, O., *Les inscriptions grecques d'Abou-Simbel*, REG, Vol. 70, 1957, pp. 1-42.

Bertherlot, K., 'The Use of Greek and Roman Stereotypes of the Egyptians by Hellenistic Jewish Apologists, with special reference to Josephus' *Against Apion*', in: Kalms, J., (ed.), *Internationals Josephus-Kolloquium*, Aarhus, 1999, pp. 185-221.

Bettalli, M., *I Mercenari nel mondo Greco*, Parte I: 'L'età arcarica', 1995.

Boardman J., *Early Greek Vase Painting: 11th-6th centuries BCE*, 1998.

Brandt, R., *The Gigantomachia in Greek Vase-Painting and Sculpture from the Middle of the Sixth to the Beginning of the Fourth Century BCE.*, Ph.D Thesis, Oxford, 1974, 1988.

Burkert, W., *The Orientalizing Revolution: Near Eastern Influence on Greek Culture in the Early Archaic Age*, 1992.

Carr, E. H., *What is History?* 1962.

Cross, F. M., 'Inscriptions in Phoenician and other Scripts', in: Stager, L. E. et al. (eds.), *Ashqelon 1: Introduction and Overview (1985-2006)*, 2008, pp. 333-372.

Deem, S., '...and the Stone Sank into His Forehead'. A Note on 1 Samuel XVII 49', *VT*, Vol. 28, Fasc. 3, 1978, 349-351.

Dossin, G., *Syria*, Vol. 19, 1938, pp. l09 f., and *Mélanges Dussaud*, II, 1939, p. 981 n. 1.

Ducrey, P., *Warfare in Ancient Greece*, trans. by J. Lloyd, 1986.

Doukelis, P. N., 'Between Greek Colony and Mother-city: Some Reflections', in: Rosen, M., (ed.), pp. 93-106.

Eph'al, I., 'Western Minorities in Babylonia in the 6th-5th centuries B.C.: Maintenance and Cohesion', *Or*, Vol. 74, 1978, pp. 74-90.

Fantalkin, A., 'Identities in Making: Greeks in the Eastern Mediterranean in the Iron Age', in: Villing, A., & Schlotzhauer, U., (eds.), pp. 199-208.

Fantalkin, A., 'Mesad Hashavyahu: Its Material Culture and Historical Background', *Tel Aviv*, 2008, no. 28, pp. 3-165.

Fantalkin, A., 'Why did Nebuchadnezzar II destroy Ashqelon in Kislev 604 BCE?', Seminar, December 29, 2009, Haifa University. (Hebrew).

Finkelstein, I., 'The Philistines in the Bible: A Late-Monarchic Perspective', *JSOT*, Vol. 27, 2002, pp. 131-167.

Finkelstein, I. & Silberman, N. A., *The Bible Unearthed*, 2003. (Hebrew).

Finkelstein, I. & Silberman, N. A., *David and Solomon: In Search of the Bible's Sacred Kings and the Roots of the Western Tradition*, 2006. (Hebrew).

Finkelstein, I., 'The Persian Period – Some Skeptical Remarks', in: *The Persian Period: Text and Context*, Symposium, May 19, 2011, Tel Aviv University.

Frazer, P. M. & Matthews, E., *Lexicon of Greek Persona Names*, Vols. I-IV, 1987.

Freedy, K. S. & Redford, D. B., 'The Dates in Ezekiel in Relation to the Biblical, Babylonian and Egyptian Sources', *JAOS*, Vol. 90, 1970, pp. 462–485.

Funkenstein, A., *Perceptions of Jewish History from the Antiquity to the Present*. 1991. (Hebrew).

Garfinkel, Y., & Ganor, S., 'Horvat Qeiafa: The Fortification of the Border of the Kingdom of Judah', in: *The Ancient Battle Field in the Land of Israel and the Surrounding Countries – Historical and Archaeological Aspects*, proceedings of January 24, 2008. (Hebrew). http://www.antiquities.org.il/article_Item_ido.asp?sec_id=17&sub_subj_id=491&id=1318#as http://www.antiquities.org.il/article_heb.aspx?sec_id=25&subj_id=240&id=2012 18 July 2013 (Hebrew).

Galil, G., *Israel and Assyria*, 2001. (Hebrew).

Galling, K., 'Goliath und seine rüstung', *VT Sup*, 15, 1966.

Garbini, G., *I Filistei: Gli antagonisti di Israele*, 1997.

Garsiel, M., ''Elements of History and Reality in the Description of the Ela Valley Warfare and the Combat Between David and Goliath (1 Sam 17)'', in: Shmuelevitz, A., 2007, pp. 4-23. (Hebrew). With slights changes of his article, 'Elements of History and Reality in the Description of the Ela Valley Warfare and the Combat Between David and Goliath (1 Sauel 17)', *Beith Mikra*, Vol. 41, 1997, pp. 293-316. (Hebrew).

Garsiel, M., ''The Elah Valley's Battle, the Duel of David and Goliath and why Goliath's Head and weapons end up in Jerusalem'', *New Studies on Jerusalem*, Vol. 14, 2008, pp. 53-87. (Hebrew).

Hanson, V. D., (ed.), *The Classical Greek Battle Experience,* 1991.

Hanson, V. D., 'Hoplite Technology in Phalanx Battle', in: Hanson, V. D., (ed.), pp. 63-86.

Hanson, V. D., *The Western Way of War: Infantry Battle in Classical Greece*, 1994.

Harrison, T., 'Crossroads of Civilization; Archaeological Explorations in the Amuq Plain. The Tayinat Archaeological Project: Temples, Palaces and Tablets', in: *The Amuq plain and the 'Land Of Palastine', Irene Levi-Sala Annual Research Seminar,* 29 March 2012, Ben Gurion University.

Hawkins, J., 'Cilicia, Amuq and Aleppo: New Light in a Dark Age', *NEA*, Vol. 72, 4, 2009, pp. 164-173.

Heard, C., "Yadin on 'David and Goliath', VT, 54, 2004', *Higgaion*, 28 April 2006. http://www.heardworld.com/higgaion/?p=398.

Heltzer, M., 'Akkadian katinnu and Hebrew kidon 'sword'', *Journal of Cuneiform Studies*, Vol. 41, 1989, pp. 65-68.

Helzer, M., 'Bn 'nt w?mgr bn-'nt (Ben-'Anat and Shamgar Ben-'Anat)', '*Al-happereq*, Vol. 8, 1994, pp. 46-49. (Hebrew).

Hockmann, U. & Moller, A., 'The Helleneion at Naukratis: Questions and Observations', in: Villing A., & Schlotzhauer, U., (eds.), pp. 11-22.

Hoffman, Y., 'The Concept of 'Other Gods' in Deuteronomistic Literature', in: Reventlow, H., Hoffman, Y., & Uffenheimer, B., (eds.), pp. 66-84.

Hoffman, Y., 'Reflections on the Relationship between Theopolitics, Profecy and Historiography', in: Reventlow, H., Hoffman, Y., & Uffenheimer, B., (eds.), pp. 85-99.

Hoffman, Y., *Jeremiah, Introduction and Commentary*, 2001. (Hebrew).

Hoffman, Y. 'Jeremiah 50-51 and the Concept of Evil in the Hebrew Bible', in: Reventlow, H., & Hoffman, Y., (eds.), *The Problem of Evil and its Symbols in Jewish and Christian Tradition*, (*JSOTSup* 366; London and New York), 2004, pp. 14-28.

Hoffmeier, J., 'Where Can Wisdom Be Found? The Sage's Language in the Bible and in Ancient Egyptian Literature' (Book review), *HSJ*, 1997, Vol. 38, p.159 (4).

Hoffmeier, J., 'David's Triumph over Goliath: 1 Samuel 17:54 and Ancient Near Eastern Analogues', in: Bar, S., Shirley, J., & Kahn, D., (eds.), *Egypt, Canaan and Israel: History, Imperialism, Ideology and Literature*, 2011, pp. 87-114.

Honeyman, A. M., 'The Evidence for Regnal Names among the Hebrews', *JBL*, Vol. LXVII, 1948, pp. 13-25.

Isaac, B., *The Invention of Racism in Classical Antiquity*, 2004.

Jafet, S., 'The Book of Chronicles: A history', *Shnaton, An Annual for Biblical and Ancient Near Eastern*, Vol. 14, 2004, pp. 101-117. (Hebrew).

Jafet, S., 'Late Biblical Historiography – How and Why?', in: *The Literature of the Bible: Introduction and studies*, Vol. 1, 2011, pp. 391-416. (Hebrew).

James, P., 'The Use and Presentation of Cultural Material in a non-Encyclopedic, General Ancient Greek Lexicon', Cambridge Greek Lexicon Project, 2009. (Greek).

Kaduri, Y., 'The Rise of the Modern Biblical Scholarship', in: T*he Literature of the Bible: Introduction and studies*, Vol. 1, 2011, pp. 3-35. (Hebrew).

Kahn, D., 'Judean Auxiliaries in Egypt's Wars against Kush', *JAOS*, Vol. 127, no. 4, 2007, pp. 507-516.

Kahn, D., 'Some Remarks on the Foreign Policy of Psammetichus II in the Levant (595-589 B.C.)', *JEH*, Vol. 1, No. 1, 2008, pp. 139-157.

Kaplan, P., 'Cross-Cultural Contacts among Mercenary Communities in Saite and Persian Egypt', *MHR*, Vol.18, No.1, 2003, pp.1–31.

Kaplan, P., 'The Social Status of the Mercenary in Archaic Greece', in: Gorman, V. B., & Robinson, E. W., (eds.), *Oikistes: Studies in Constitutions, Colonies, and Military Power in the Ancient World*, 2002, pp. 229-243.

Kasher, A., 'Political and National Connections between the Jews of Ptolemaic Egypt and Their Brethren in Eretz Israel', in: Oppenheimer, A., & Kasher, A., (eds.), *From Generation to Generation: From the End of the Biblical Period to the Sealing of the Talmud. Collection of Researches in Honor of Joshua Ephron*, 1995. (Hebrew).

Kasher, A., 'A Jewish *Politeuma* in Alexandria: A Pattern of Jewish Communal Life in a Greco-Roman Diaspora', in: Rosen, M., (ed.), pp. 109-125.
Kirk, G. S., *The Iliad: A Complementary*, Vol. II: Books 5-8, 1990.
Kitchen, K. A., *Ancient Orient and Old Testament*, 1966, pp. 85-86.
Kletter, R., 'Weighing and weights in Eretz Israel in antiquity', *Etmol*, Vol. 3, no. 155, 2001. (Hebrew).
Knapp, R., 'Greek Coinage, Mercenaries, and Ideology', *Eulimene*, Vol. 3, 2002, pp. 183-196.
Krentz, P., 'Warfare and Hoplites', in: Shapiro, H. A., (ed.), *Archaic Greece*, 2007, pp. 61-84.
Küçükeren, C. C., *An Anatolian Civilization in the Aegean Karia*, 2005.
Kurke, L., 'Crisis and Decorum in Sixth-Century Lesbos: Reading Alkaios Otherwise', *Quaderni Urbinati di Cultura Classica*, Vol. 47, No. 2, 1994, pp. 67-92.
Leaf, W., *The Iliad, Vol. 1: Books 1-4*, 1960.
Liddell, H. G., & Scott, R., *Greek-English Lexicon*, 1985.
LIMC, Vol. IV, 1988, figs. 1-443.
Liphschits, O., 'A New Outlook on the Archaeology of Persian Period Yehud', in: *The Persian Period: Text and Context*, Symposium, May 19, 2011, Tel Aviv University.
Lipinski, E., *On the Skirts of Canaan in the Iron Age*, 2006.
Livingston, L., 'Egyptian Influence on Ionic Temple Architecture', in: *Special Studies: Directed Research Project, University of Notre Dame*, 2000. www.artic.edu/~ livin/ research/ionic…/paper.html
Luckenbill, D. D., *Ancient Records of Assyria and Babylonia*, 2 Vols., 1927.
Luraghi, N., 'Traders, Pirates, Warriors: The Proto-History of Greek Mercenary Soldiers in the Eastern Mediterranean', *Phoenix*, Vol. 60, no.1/2, 2006, pp. 21-47.
Macalister, R. A. S., *The Philistines: Their History and Civilization*, 1965.
Mack, A., et al. 'Perceptual organization and attention', *Cognitive Psychology*, Vol. 24, no. 4, 1992, pp. 475-501.
Maeir, A. M., Wimmer, S. J., Zuckerman, A., & Demski, A., 'A Late Iron Age I/Early Iron Age II Old Canaanite Inscription from Tell es-safi/Gath, Israel: Palaeography, Dating, and Historical-Cultural Significance', *BASOR*, Vol. 351, 2008, pp. 39-71.
Malamat, A., 'Three Models of Early Israeli Warfare', in: Shmuelevitz, A., (ed.), pp. 11-21 (Hebrew).
Malkin, I., *The Returns of Odysseus: Colonization and Ethnicity*, 2004. (Hebrew).
Malkin, I., 'Networks and the Emergence of Greek Identity', *MHR*, Vol. 18, no. 2, 2003, pp. 56-74.
Malkin, I., 'Pan Hellenism and the Greeks of Naukratis', in: Reddé, M., (ed.), *Naissance de la ville dans l'antiquité*, 2003, pp. 91-95.
Malkin, I., *A Small Greek World*, 2011.
Margalith, O., *The Sea People in the Bible*, 1994.
Mayerson, P., *Classical mythology in literature, art, and music*, 2001, p. 68.
McNutt, P., *The Forging of Israel: Iron Technology, Symbolism and Tradition in Ancient Israel*, 1990.
Mélèze Modrzejewski, J., *The Jews of Egypt: from Ramses II to Emperor Hadrian*, 1995.
Moore, M. B., 'The Central Group in the Gigantomachy of the Old Athena Temple on the Acropolis', *AJA*, Vol. 99, No. 4, 1995, pp. 633-639.

Morgan, C., 'Symbolic and Pragmatic Aspects of Warfare in the Greek World of the 8th to the 6th Centuries BC', in: Bekker-Nielsen, T., & Hannestad, L., (eds.), pp. 20-44.

Murray, O., *Early Greece*, 2001.

Na'aman, N., 'The Negev in the Last Century of the Kingdom of Judah', *Qatedra*, Vol. 42, 1987, pp. 4-15. (Hebrew).

Na'aman, N., 'The Kingdom of Judah under Joshia', *Tel Aviv*, Vol. 18, 1991, pp. 1-69.

Na'aman, N., *The Past that Shapes the Present. The Creation of Biblical Historiography in the Late First Temple Period and after the Downfall*, Yeriot, Vol. 3, 2002. (Hebrew).

Na'aman, N., 'In Search of the Ancient Name of *KHIRBET QEIYAFA*', *JHS*, Vol. 8, article 21, 2008, pp.1-8.

Na'aman, N., 'Historiography in the Former Prophets', in: Talshir, Z., (ed.), *The Literature of the Bible: Introduction and studies*, Vol. 1, 2011, pp. 371-390. (Hebrew).

Naveh, J., 'Writings and scripts in Seventh-Century B.C.E. Philistia: The New Evidence from Tell Jemmeh', *IEJ*, Vol. 35, 1985, pp. 8-21.

Naveh, J., 'Mesad Hashavyahu', in: Stern, E., (ed.), Vol. 2, pp. 557-558. (Hebrew).

Nielsen, A.J. F., *The Tragedy in History: Herodotus and the Deuteronomist History*, JSOTSup ; 251. Clines, D., & Davis, P., (eds.), 1997.

Niemier, W. D., 'Archaic Greeks in the Orient: Textual and Archaeological Evidence', *BASOR*, Vol. 322, 2001, pp. 11-32.

Noth, M., *The History of Israel*, 1960.

Oded, B., 'The Settlements of the Israelite and the Judean Exiles in Mesopotamia in the 8th-6th Centuries BCE', in Galil, G., & Weinfeld, M., (eds.), *Studies in Historical Geography and Biblical Historiography Presented to Zecharia Kallai*, VTSup, no. 81, 2000, pp. 91-103.

Oded, B., 'Exile – The Biblical Perspectives', in: Rosen, M., (ed.), pp. 85-92.

Oren, E., 'Sinai', in: Stern, E., (ed.), *The New Encyclopedia of Archaeological Excavations in the Holy Land*, 1992, Vol. 3, pp. 1111-1113. (Hebrew).

Ornan, T., *The Triumph of the Symbol. Pictorial Representation of Deities in Mesopotamia and the Biblical Image Ban*, 2005.

Papansatasiou, G., 'The Presentation ΣYN in Ancient Greek Compounds', 2011, pp. 366-378. http://www.scribd.com/doc/48260735/papanastassiouICGL8

Parke, H. W., *The Oracles of Apollo in Asia Minor*, 1985.

Petrie, W. F. M., *The Palace of Apries (MEMPHIS 11)*, 1909.

Porten, B., *Archives from Elephantine :the life of an ancient Jewish military colony*, 1968.

Pritchett, W. C., *The Greek State at War*, part IV, 1985.

Quirke, S., *Ancient Egyptian Religion*, 1996.

Raaflaub, K. A., 'Archaic Greek Aristocrats as Carriers of Cultural Interaction', in: Rollinger, R., & Ulf, C., (eds.), *Commerce and monetary systems in the ancient world :means of transmission and cultural interaction : proceedings of the Fifth Annual Symposium of the Assyrian and Babylonian Intellectual Heritage Project, Innsbruck, Austria, October 3rd-8th 2002*, 2004.

Raaflaub, K. A., & Van Wees, H., (eds.), *A Companion to Archaic Greece,* 2009.

Ray, J., 'Soldiers to Pharaoh: The Carians of Southwest Anatolia', in: Sasson, J. M., (ed.), *Civilizations of the Ancient Near East*, Vol. 2, 1995, pp. 1185-1194.

Reventlow, H., Hoffman, Y., & Uffenheimer, B., (eds.), *Politics and Theopolitics in the Bible and Postbiblical Literature*, 1994.

Rofé, A., 'Jeremiah and His Book: Words of Summary', *Beit Mikra*, Vol. 3, no. 4, 1986, p. 107. (Hebrew).

Rofé, A., 'Promise and Desertion – Eretz Israel and the Beginning of the Commonwealth', *Qatedra*, Vol. 41, 1986, pp. 3-10. (Hebrew).

Rofé, A., 'The Battle of David and Goliath: Folklore, Theology, Eschatology', *Eshel Beer Sheva – Studies in Jewish Thought*, Vol. 3, 1986, pp. 55-89. (Hebrew).

Rofé, A., *The Prophetical Stories: The Narratives about the Prophets in the Hebrew Bible, Their Literary Types and History*, 1986. (Hebrew).

Rofé, A., *Introduction to the Literature of the Hebrew Bible*, 2006. (Hebrew).

Rosen, M., 'People of the Book, People of the Sea: Mirror Images of the Soul', in: Rosen, M., (ed.), pp. 35-81.

Rosen, M., (ed.), *Homelands and Diasporas: Greeks, Jews and their Migrations*, 2008.

Safrai, S., *Pilgrimage at the Time of the Second Temple*, 1965. (Hebrew).

Schwartz, D., 'The Jews of Egypt between the Temple of Onias, the Temple of Jerusalem, and Heaven', *Zion*, Vol. 62, no.1, 1997, pp. 5-22. (Hebrew).

Schipper, B., 'Egyptian Imperialism after the New Kingdom. The 26th Dynasty and the Southern Levant', in: Bar, S., Shirley, J., & Kahn, D., (eds.), *Egypt, Canaan and Israel: History, Imperialism, Ideology and Literature*, 2011, pp. 269-290.

Shmuelevitz, A., (ed.), *The Battlefield: Decisive Battles in the Land of Israel*, 2007. (Hebrew).

Shupak, N., *Where can Wisdom be found? The Sage's Language in the Bible and the Ancient Egyptian Literature.* 1993.

Singer, I., 'Toward an Image of Dagon, the God of the Philistines', *Qatedra*, Vol. 54, 1989, pp. 17-42. (Hebrew).

Singer, I., 'The Philistines in the Bible: A Reflection of the Late-Monarchic Period', *Zemanim*, Vol. 94, 2006, pp. 74-82. (Hebrew).

Singer, I., *The Hittites and their Culture*, 2009. (Hebrew).

Smith, A. C., 'From Drunkenness to a Hangover: Maenads as Personifications', in: Herrin, J., & Stafford, J., (eds.), *Personification In The Greek World: From Antiquity To Byzantium*, 2005, pp. 211-230.

Smith-Christopher, D. L., *The Religion of the Landless*, 1989.

Smith-Christopher, D. L., *A Biblical Theology of Exile (Overtures to Biblical Theology)*, 2002.

Snodgrass, A. M., *Arms and Armour of the Greeks*, 1967.

Snodgrass, A. M., *Archaeology and the Emergence of Greece*, 2006.

Snodgrass, A. M., *Early Greek Armour and Weapon from the End of the Bronze Age to 600 B.C.*, 1964.

Sullivan, B., 'Paying Archaic Greek Mercenaries: Views from Egypt and the Near East', *The Classical Journal*, Vol. 107, No. 1, 2011, pp. 31-61.

Tadmor, H., 'Historical Implications of the Correct Rendering of Akkadian dāku', *JNES*, Vol. 17, 1958, pp. 129-131.

Tadmor, H., 'Rab Sāris and Rab Shakeh in 2 Kings 18', in: Meyers, C., & O'Connor, M., (eds.), *The Word of the Lord Shall Go Forth: Essays in Honor of David Noel Freedman*, 1983, pp. 279-285.

Thompson, D., *Memphis under the Ptolemies*, 1988.

Thompson, T. L., *Early History of the Israelite People. From the Written and Archaeological Sources*, 1992.

Tov, E., 'Jeremiah', 'Ezekiel', in: Galil, G., (ed.), *The World of the Bible*, 1990. (Hebrew).

Trundle, M., 'Identity and Community among Greek Mercenaries in the Classical World: 700-322 BCE', *AHB*, Vol. 13, no. 1, 1999, pp. 28-38.

Trundle, M., *Greek Mercenaries: From the Late Archaic Period to Alexander*, 2004.

Ussishkin, D., *The conquest of Lachish by Sennacherib*, 1982.

Van Wees, H., 'The Homeric Way of War: the Iliad and the Hoplite Phalanx (II)', *Greece & Rome*, Vol. xli, no. 2, 1994, pp. 131-155.

Van Wees, H., 'The Myth of the Middle Class Army: military and social status in ancient Athens', in: Bekker-Nielsen, T., & Hannestad, L., (eds.), pp. 45-71.

Vaughn, P., 'The Identification and Retrieval of the Hoplite Battle-Dead', in: Hanson, V. D., (ed.), pp. 38-62.

Vaux, R. de, *The Early History of Israel*, 1978.

Villing, A., & Schlotzhauer, U., (eds.), *Naukratis: Greek Diversity in Egypt*, 2006.

Villing, A., & Schlotzhauer, U., 'Naukratis and the Eastern Mediterranean: Past, Present and Future', in: Villing, A., & Schlotzhauer, U., (eds.), pp. 1-10.

Wheeler, E. L., 'The General as a Hoplite', in: Hanson, V. D., (ed.), pp. 121-172.

Wiesehöfer, J., 'The Persian Empire and Yehud', in: *The Persian Period: Text and Context*, Symposium, May 19, 2011, Tel Aviv University.

Williams, D., & Villing, A., 'Carian Mercenaries at Naukratis?' in: Villing, A., & Schlotzhauer, U., (eds.), pp. 47-48.

Winckler, H., *Altorientalische Forschungen*, 1897.

Wiseman, D. J., *Chronicles of Chaldaean kings (626-556 B. C.) in the British Museum*, 1956.

Wiseman, D. J., *Nebuchadrezar and Babylon*, 1991.

Yadin, A., 'Goliath's Armour and Israelite Collective Memory', *VT*, Vol. 54, Fasc. 3, 2004, pp. 373-395.

Yankelevitz, R., 'The Temple of Onias - Law and Reality', in: Oppenheimer, A., Gafni, I., & Stern, M., (eds.), *in the Second Temple, Mishna and Talmud Period*, 1993, pp. 107-115. (Hebrew).

Yasur-Landau, A., *The Philistines and the Aegean Migration*, 2010.

Yasur-Landau, A., 'Sea Peoples and Neo-Hittites in the 'Land of Palistin'' in: *The Amuq plain and the 'Land Of Palastine', Irene Levi-Sala Annual Research Seminar*, 29 March 2012, Ben Gurion University.

Yavetz, Z., *Then and Now: Studies, Essays, Lectures*, Vols. 1-3, 2002. (Hebrew).

Yoyotte, J., & Masson, O., *Objects pharaoniques a inscription carienne*, 1956.

Wiesehöfer, J., 'The Persian Empire and Yehud', in: *The Persian Period: Text and Context*, Symposium, May 19, 2011, Tel Aviv University.

Wilson, P., 'Consolidation, Innovation, and Renaissance', in: Wendrich, W., (ed.), *Egyptian Archaeology*, 2010, pp. 241-258.

Zadok, R., 'Phoenicians, Philistines and Moabites in Mesopotamia in the First Millennium B.C.', *BASOR*, Vol. 230, 1978, pp. 57-65.

Zadok, R., 'On Anatolians, Greeks and Egyptians in 'Chaldean' and Achaemenid Babylonia', *Tel Aviv*, Vol. 32, 2005, pp. 76-106.

Zakovitch, Y., & Shinan, A., *That's Not What the Good Book Says*, 2004. (Hebrew).

Zertal, A., *Sisra's Secret*, 2010. (Hebrew).

Zivie-Coche, C., 'Late Period Temples', in: Willeke Wendrich (ed.), *Encyclopedia of Egyptology*, 2008, pp. 1-18. http://escholarship.org/uc/item/30k472wh.

Abbreviations

AASOR	Annual of the American Schools of Oriental Research
AHB	Ancient History Bulletin
AJA	American Journal of Archaeology
BASOR	Bulletin of the American Schools of Oriental Research
HSJ	Hebrew Studies Journal
IEJ	Israel Exploration Journal
JAOS	Journal of the American Oriental Society
JBL	Journal of Biblical Literature
JEH	Journal of Egyptian History
JHS	Journal of Hebrew Scriptures
JNES	Journal of Near Eastern Studies
JSOT	Journal for the Study of the Old Testament
JSOTSup	Journal for the Study of the Old Testament Suppliment Series
MHR	Mediterranean Historical Review
NEA	Near Eastern Archeology
Or	Orientalia
REG	Revue des Études Grecques
VT	Vetus Testamentum